Mary
Queen of Angels

ALSO BY DOREEN VIRTUE

Books/Kits/Oracle Board

Assertiveness for Earth Angels (available March 2013)
The Miracles of Archangel Gabriel (available October 2012)
Mermaids 101 (available September 2012)
Flower Therapy (with Robert Reeves; available August 2012)
Saved by an Angel
The Angel Therapy® Handbook
Angel Words (with Grant Virtue)
Archangels 101
The Healing Miracles of Archangel Raphael
The Art of Raw Living Food (with Jenny Ross)
Signs from Above (with Charles Virtue)
The Miracles of Archangel Michael
Angel Numbers 101
Solomon's Angels (a novel)
My Guardian Angel (with Amy Oscar)
Angel Blessings Candle Kit (with Grant Virtue;
includes booklet, CD, journal, etc.)
Thank You, Angels! (children's book with Kristina Tracy)
Healing Words from the Angels
How to Hear Your Angels
Realms of the Earth Angels
Fairies 101
Daily Guidance from Your Angels
Divine Magic
How to Give an Angel Card Reading Kit
Angels 101
Angel Guidance Board
Goddesses & Angels
Crystal Therapy (with Judith Lukomski)
Connecting with Your Angels Kit
(includes booklet, CD, journal, etc.)
Angel Medicine
The Crystal Children
Archangels & Ascended Masters
Earth Angels
Messages from Your Angels
Angel Visions II
Eating in the Light (with Becky Prelitz, M.F.T., R.D.)
The Care and Feeding of Indigo Children
Healing with the Fairies
Angel Visions
Divine Prescriptions
Healing with the Angels
"I'd Change My Life If I Had More Time"
Divine Guidance
Chakra Clearing
Angel Therapy®
The Lightworker's Way
Constant Craving A–Z
Constant Craving
The Yo-Yo Diet Syndrome
Losing Your Pounds of Pain

Audio/CD Programs

Angel Therapy® Meditations
Archangels 101 (abridged audio book)
Fairies 101 (abridged audio book)
Goddesses & Angels (abridged audio book)
Angel Medicine (available as both 1- and 2-CD sets)
Angels among Us (with Michael Toms)
Messages from Your Angels (abridged audio book)
Past-Life Regression with the Angels
Divine Prescriptions
The Romance Angels
Connecting with Your Angels
Manifesting with the Angels
Karma Releasing
Healing Your Appetite, Healing Your Life
Healing with the Angels
Divine Guidance
Chakra Clearing

DVD Program

How to Give an Angel Card Reading

Oracle Cards (divination cards and guidebook)

Indigo Angel Oracle Cards (with Charles Virtue; available July 2013)
Angel Dreams Oracle Cards (with Melissa Virtue; available March 2013)
Mary, Queen of Angels Oracle Cards (available November 2012)
Angel Tarot Cards (with Radleigh Valentine and Steve A. Roberts)
The Romance Angels Oracle Cards
Life Purpose Oracle Cards
Archangel Raphael Healing Oracle Cards
Archangel Michael Oracle Cards
Angel Therapy® Oracle Cards
Magical Messages from the Fairies Oracle Cards
Ascended Masters Oracle Cards
Daily Guidance from Your Angels Oracle Cards
Saints & Angels Oracle Cards
Magical Unicorns Oracle Cards
Goddess Guidance Oracle Cards
Archangel Oracle Cards
Magical Mermaids and Dolphins Oracle Cards
Messages from Your Angels Oracle Cards
Healing with the Fairies Oracle Cards
Healing with the Angels Oracle Cards

All of the above are available at your local bookstore,
or may be ordered by visiting:

Hay House UK: **www.hayhouse.co.uk**;
Hay House USA: **www.hayhouse.com**®;
Hay House Australia: **www.hayhouse.com.au**;
Hay House South Africa: **www.hayhouse.co.za**;
Hay House India: **www.hayhouseco.in**

Doreen's website: **www.AngelTherapy.com**

DOREEN VIRTUE

HAY HOUSE

Australia • Canada • Hong Kong • India
South Africa • United Kingdom • United States

First published and distributed in the United Kingdom by:
Hay House UK Ltd, 292B Kensal Rd, London W10 5BE. Tel.: (44) 20 8962
1230; Fax: (44) 20 8962 1239. www.hayhouse.co.uk

Published and distributed in the United States of America by:
Hay House, Inc., PO Box 5100, Carlsbad, CA 92018-5100. Tel.: (1) 760 431
7695 or (800) 654 5126; Fax: (1) 760 431 6948 or (800) 650 5115.
www.hayhouse.com

Published and distributed in Australia by:
Hay House Australia Ltd, 18/36 Ralph St, Alexandria NSW 2015.
Tel.: (61) 2 9669 4299; Fax: (61) 2 9669 4144. www.hayhouse.com.au

Published and distributed in the Republic of South Africa by:
Hay House SA (Pty), Ltd, PO Box 990, Witkoppen 2068.
Tel./Fax: (27) 11 467 8904. www.hayhouse.co.za

Published and distributed in India by:

Hay House   , Vasant
Kunj, New D   176 1630.

Rair   .

T

Cover a   *lch*

A catalogue record for this book is available from the British Library.

ISBN 978-1-84850-454-7

Printed and bound in Great Britain by
TJ International, Padstow, Cornwall.

*To Mother Mary,
Queen of the Angels*

CONTENTS

Introduction xi

Chapter 1: Seeing the Beloved Mother in Visions
and Dreams 1

Chapter 2: Mother Mary Physical Healings 21

Chapter 3: Mother Mary Emotional Healings 37

Chapter 4: Children and Mother Mary 53

Chapter 5: Mary Motherhood 77

Chapter 6: Protected by Mother Mary 89

Chapter 7: Prayers to the Beloved Mother 99

Chapter 8: Purposeful Careers and Abundant Supply 107

Chapter 9: Signs from Mother Mary 117

Chapter 10: Mother Mary Statues 127

Chapter 11: Roses from Heaven 133

Chapter 12: Sites of Marian Visions and Worship 147

Appendix

• Biblical References to Mother Mary 159

• Modern Prayers to Mother Mary 165

• Traditional Catholic Mother Mary Prayers,
Novena, and Liturgies 171

Acknowledgments 189

About the Author 191

INTRODUCTION

This is a nondenominational book about the beautiful, loving, and sacred Mother Mary. I've endeavored to write it so that it's inclusive of established religion, as well as paths that are more spiritual than religious. I take the topic of Mother Mary very seriously, with great respect and awe for her and the traditions surrounding her.

In writing this book, I've spent much time in prayer and research so that I could present it with the love and the maternal caring that are the heart of Mother Mary herself. It has been a labor of love, as well as an opportunity for me to explore the topic of Mother Mary for myself and pass what I've discovered on to you.

Mary, Queen of Angels doesn't analyze controversial issues or interpret scripture, as there are plenty of works that serve those purposes. Instead, it is an exploration of the experiences of those who have found themselves in the presence of the Beloved Mother through prayers, visitations, apparitions, dreams, and healings. I'm not a Catholic, which is the religion most associated with the figure of Mary. However, I'm passionate about Mother Mary and her healing presence. During my extensive international travels, I always seek out cathedrals and basilicas devoted to the Blessed Mother. I've visited Lourdes, France; the Holy House within the Loreto Cathedral, Italy; and countless other cathedrals dedicated to her.

Additionally, I've studied the Catholic religion's history and tenets since my early days in college, and have great respect for its mysteries and miracles. I consider myself an open-minded Christian, meaning that my primary foundation is with Jesus, and I also find value and blessings in many spiritual paths. I focus upon the aspects of love, forgiveness, compassion, charity, and ethics from the different religions, and bypass the fear and guilt.

In this book, I'm not advocating worshipping Mother Mary above God, in the same way that I never promote the worship of angels (the topic of many of my other books). God is the All-in-All Whom we worship. Since the Creator is omnipresent, Mother Mary and the angels are one with God in spiritual truth.

The devotion to Mother Mary is increasing at a time when the congregation numbers are declining among traditional religions, and people are restlessly seeking spiritual truth. Those who are students of world religions and cultures are familiar with feminine deities within polytheistic (many-god) pantheons. Mother Mary fits that need for the Divine Sacred Feminine within the monotheistic (one-God) paradigm.

If you've had negative experiences with religion, I feel great compassion for what you've endured. I also understand that some aspects of this book may inadvertently trigger old feelings. My prayer is that reading it will lead to healing. I do understand the deep wounds arising from hearing that you're a sinner or other teachings that promote low self-esteem, fear, and guilt. I also understand that abusive personalities cause pain within many organizations, including religious ones. Yet, there are aspects of each religion worth keeping, including the power of prayer and the connection to the sacred.

The Story of Mary

Mary is the most prominent female figure in Christianity, yet she is only mentioned in the Gospels a few times (please see "Biblical References to Mother Mary," in this book's Appendix). As the mother of Jesus, she is accorded great reverence, even with the controversies surrounding the Immaculate Conception. Mary, the Madonna, is central to monotheistic traditions. She is discussed in Islamic literature as the only named female in the Qur'an, and sainted in Catholicism and Orthodox churches. The name Mary appears 51 times in the New Testament, referring to at least nine different women.

Mary is the daughter of Anne and Joachim, according to the noncanonical Book of James. Anne (also known as Hannah) and Joachim (sometimes called Imran) are both believed to be of King David's lineage. The couple were having difficulty conceiving their firstborn child, so they prayed for assistance. Angels appeared and promised them a child. Soon after, Mary was born. So the Queen of Angels was heralded by an angelic visitation to her parents. Mary's cousin, Elizabeth (daughter of her mother's sister), was also visited by the archangel Gabriel, who announced the birth of her son, John the Baptist. He later went to Mary and said, "Behold, I bring you good tidings of great joy," and proceeded to describe her future son, Jesus Christ.

Although Mother Mary is associated with Catholicism, Christianity, and Orthodox traditions, she and Jesus were themselves of the Jewish faith and culture. Mary—like Jesus and the angels, and especially God—belongs to all faiths, all religions, all paths, and all people. They are pure love, which is inclusive . . . without judgment, jealousy, or competitiveness.

Mother Mary is our ideal parent: sweet, pure, nurturing, unconditionally loving, accepting, humble, wise, understanding, and compassionate. She comforts us with a soothing knowingness that puts our minds at rest. She reassures troubled hearts and allows us to feel loved and safe. She helps us to trust and believe in fairness and goodness.

Writing this book deepened my relationship with Mother Mary, in discovering the many ways in which she is protecting, healing, and guiding us all. She cares for each and every inhabitant of our planet, as well as for the earth itself. She's unlimited in her ability to help and heal everyone simultaneously.

Mother Mary is a role model of balance (especially for women), as the nurturing giver who is also wise and strong. She exhibits the necessity and value of self-care, even as she gives everything to those she loves.

I grew up with the Christmas story from the book of Luke, with its enchanting description of Archangel Gabriel announcing the forthcoming birth of Jesus to Mother Mary. I loved hearing about Mary's journey with her husband, Joseph, to Bethlehem, culminating in the nativity and the world-changing heralding of Jesus the Savior.

When I visited Lourdes in the south of France, I also experienced the power of Mother Mary's love. I watched as the sick on gurneys were wheeled by medical attendants to the Lourdes well, surrounded by hundreds of lit white candles and praying people. And then when I got close to the well, I felt as if I'd touched heaven itself and walked through a purifying waterfall of angels.

Later, when I had the opportunity to spend time at the Loreto Cathedral in Italy, I began crying at the amount of love I felt there. The story behind this site is that during the Crusades the Holy Home where Mary was born and received the Annunciation was moved to protect it from destruction. Some even say that angels flew the house to Italy to safeguard it. It was reassembled in the town of Loreto, and later a basilica was built around it.

Historians can't agree upon the validity of the Holy Home story. However, apparently the structure was carbondated, and it was deemed plausible that it could be from the Holy Land in the approximate time frame of Jesus and his family. After 2,000 years of people's prayers inside, I was bowled over by the sacred beauty of the experience and reduced to tears.

Different Names for Mary

Mother Mary is called the "Queen of the Angels" because she's considered the feminine overseer of heaven, which is home to the angels. She lives and works among these beings, and is herself the supreme Earth angel. She is one of the humans documented in the Bible as having a profound angel experience.

The term *Queen of Angels* is based on the vision of a sister of the Bernardine order, who saw evil harming the world. In this vision, Mary asked the sister to pray so that the Blessed Mother could dispatch Archangel Michael and other angels to send the evil away. The sister asked why we would need to pray for this action when Mary and the angels could see the evil. That's when the Beloved Mother explained that God made us with free will, and that we must pray for intervention.

Mary, like God, Jesus, and the angels, is unlimited. She's able to be with everyone simultaneously, having a unique and individual experience. She helps people of all faiths, and she answers all prayers.

She goes by many names and titles, some of them derived from church councils, several from devotional prayers, and others from Marian visitations (people being visited by Mary). She is referred to as a *tower, throne, queen,* and *virgin.* Some of Mary's other names include:

— **Mystical Rose** (or *Santa Maria della Rosa*). Mother Mary is associated with roses and the mystical legends of the rose lineage and the Holy Grail. As you'll read in this book, many people smell the fragrance of roses when they experience a healing or visitation from Mother Mary.

— **Our Lady of Guadalupe.** This name stems from the Marian visions near Mexico City, where the Basilica of Guadalupe now stands. Such visions occur around the world, and Guadalupe is among the most visited of these locations.

— **Star of the Sea** (or *Stella Maris* in Latin). Mother Mary is referred to as the protectress of sailors. Indeed, in many languages the word for ocean is *mar,* of which the name Mary is a derivative.

Honoring Mother Mary and God

In Catholicism, Mother Mary is revered with Feast Days, which are holy days on which saints and sacred events are commemorated. Mary's major Feast Day is August 1, the date when scholars believe she ascended to heaven. December 8 marks another important Feast Day called the Immaculate Conception, on which Saint Anne conceived Mary.

I'm frequently asked if it's blasphemous to pray to angels, to which I reply that angels don't want to be worshipped. They simply want to know our prayers so they may act as intercessors for God. There has been much criticism, similarly, of worshipping Mary (and other deities) and making them false idols.

I believe that Mary, like the angels, desires that all glory go to God, our Creator. We aren't honoring her above God or instead of God.

So why appeal to Mary or angels at all when you can just as easily talk directly to God? Since God is 100 percent love, the mind of the Creator only *knows* love. When your heart and mind are open with a loving outlook, you can easily hear and feel the presence of the Divine. But when you're stressed or afraid (and need God the most), your vibrations are lowered to the point where you feel distanced from the Creator. That's where Mary and the angels come in: they can match your vibrations, no matter how low you're feeling, and lift you back up to Divine love.

Mary, like the angels, is free from the fear and guilt that antagonize those who eschew religion. Many people connect to Mary through the sorrow she must have felt at her son's death, yet we all recognize that she's risen above the pain into great compassion for all who suffer. In this way, Mary is a role model and guide for turning our life's pain into useful lessons to help others.

A Note about the Stories in This Book

As I was writing this book, I asked my readers to send me their stories of experiences with the Blessed Mother. I have read and reread each story submitted, and have included those I feel represent a wide range of experiences. I am not necessarily endorsing all the viewpoints of the story authors, but am including them as I would include everyone in a group discussion about Mother Mary. My prayer is that the stories will inspire you to deepen your own connection with the Beloved Mother.

CHAPTER ONE

SEEING THE BELOVED MOTHER IN VISIONS AND DREAMS

Many people "see" the Blessed Mother while praying, meditating, or dreaming. Sometimes this image is static, like looking at a photograph or painting. Other times it involves Mother Mary moving or speaking.

The vision occurs within the mind's eye so that it is a contained experience inside the person's head. This doesn't mean, however, that the person is imagining it. The messages and feelings connected to it are so powerful and life altering that they exceed mere daydreams. These visions also may contain information that the person couldn't have previously known.

Visions differ from apparition sightings, in which Mother Mary is seen as a living and life-size person standing outside oneself. Apparition experiences are most frequent with children, but they are increasingly occurring with adults, too.

According to the Marian Library at the University of Dayton, the rise in reports of apparitions may suggest that there is a spiritual hunger today that goes beyond institutional churches. Rev. Johann Roten, a Marianist priest who directs the Marian Library–International Marian Research Institute, explains:

There's a need for the mystery to be put back in people's lives. Apparitions may be one of God's many answers to these needs. Apparitions remind us that Christianity is a religious tradition based on mediation. God is not immediately present, but he gives himself to be understood and shared. He entrusts himself or his message to Mary, who in turn entrusts this same message to the visionary who passes it on to a multitude of people. These again share the message with others.[1]

We'll look at the sacred Marian locations associated with apparitions in Chapter 12. In this chapter, the focus is on the more private and personal visions of people that helped and healed them.

My Connection to Mother Mary

My own first powerful experience with Mother Mary occurred in a vision the summer after I graduated from high school. I was living with my girlfriend Kathy and her boyfriend in a community near Palm Springs, California. We had all taken odd jobs to pay the rent and other bills. On day two of my new job as a waitress, I still bungled the diner's system of writing customer food orders for the chef, and he constantly chastised me for putting the drink orders on the wrong part of the ticket. For some reason, my brain couldn't get the hang of waitressing, and they fired me by day three.

Although the adventure of being on my own was exciting, I missed my family and felt anxious about finances and my future. Falling asleep in my darkened bedroom, I made a nonspecific prayer to God for help and guidance.

That's when I had the vision of three figures floating toward me. At first they were small and in the distance. I could see that

---

1 "The Mary Page," the Marian Library, University of Dayton: **http://campus .udayton.edu/mary**.

they were slowly coming toward me, growing progressively larger and clearer. I recognized two of the figures as Jesus Christ and Mother Mary. The third figure was male, and I still don't know his identity.

Am I dying? I wondered. *Are they coming to take me to heaven?*

I panicked, sitting up, and considered turning on my bedroom light to stop the vision. But something made me continue focusing upon the three figures, who had almost reached me now. Although I was still afraid that they were coming to escort me to heaven, I nonetheless relaxed and surrendered to the experience.

If this is God's will and my time to go, I trust it, I decided. I lay back down fully on my bed and waited for death to overtake me. As the figures neared my body, I felt huge waves of warm loving energy. I felt and saw them merge with my body, especially my heart. The thought came to me: *I've been reborn!*

This experience changed the course of my life. The next day, I made arrangements to return to my parents' home. The experience taught me that whenever we set off upon a discordant path (where things are a struggle and nothing seems to go right), we can ask God for help. I learned that this help is given in unforeseen ways, such as this healing visitation, which set me on a better life path.

Visions of Mary

Visions and apparitions of Mother Mary are on the rise, as the University of Dayton expert noted. Sometimes these experiences are shared by other people, such as the three children who saw and heard the Blessed Mother together in Fátima, Portugal, in 1917.

It was in a group vision shared by children that **Cherise Greski** experienced Mother Mary while in her teaching classroom:

Cherise has been strongly devoted to Mother Mary since she was a little girl. She said the Rosary regularly, and had a beautiful night-light with an image of the Blessed Mother on it by her bed. When she was 16, Cherise volunteered to teach a Catholic religion class on Saturdays to public-school fourth graders. She always believed and "knew" that there was more to Mother Mary and the angels than she had been taught in school. However, there was a very set curriculum to be taught, and while she attempted to follow it, her heart wasn't quite in that space.

One day Cherise was explaining to the children how we should all love God. She had them stand up and physically feel where love would be if we loved God with our whole minds (pointing above the head), our whole hearts (touching the heart), our whole bodies (she had the children breathe deeply), and our whole souls.

In the middle of her lesson, a beautiful light appeared among the students. Cherise stared intently, as this light emanated a radiance beyond anything she had ever seen and then transformed into the most beautiful woman she could imagine. She quickly looked around for a source of the light, a reflection . . . anything to explain it "logically," but she couldn't. The woman's beauty was not necessarily classical, but it was striking. Then it dawned on Cherise: *Oh my—it's Mother Mary!* Her heart soared as Mary smiled at her.

Cherise had the children sit down so they could talk about what had just happened. As soon as they did, one girl raised her hand to ask where the beautiful lady had gone.

Cherise realized that she hadn't been the only one to see the vision. She said a prayer to Mother Mary and God, asking for a way to explain what had occurred, but nothing came to her.

Instead, Cherise felt guided to invite the children to share. Putting aside the curriculum, they had a delightful class. The kids were interested, engaged, and excited about being loved, and loving God! What a wonderful class that was!

Then the students went home and shared the experience with their friends and loved ones. They rejoiced in their faith in a way they never had before.

This experience took place more than 30 years ago, yet each time Cherise shares it, the energy in her body confirming her experience is as clear, loving, and supportive as it was then. Mother Mary has been a continuing and powerful influence throughout her entire life. And often when she is in the most need of love and support, Cherise is transported to that beautiful moment three decades before.

Children are open to new experiences, without the doubts that can block adults from consciously connecting with the Divine. A child's pure faith in possibilities allows her to be aware of the spiritual world that surrounds us. Perhaps that's why, according to a 1980s study at the University of Ohio, young children have significantly more verifiable prescient experiences compared with other age-groups.

For example, Mother Mary appeared to **Theresa Falese** when she was seven years old. It was many years ago, but Theresa can still remember it as clear as day. It must have been 2 in the morning, and everyone was sleeping. Theresa saw a ball of white light coming down through the ceiling. Then a beautiful woman appeared. She was dressed in blue and white and had long dark hair. Theresa remembers that she was barefoot, and her feet didn't touch the floor.

Theresa shared a room with her sister, who was fast asleep. She called out for her parents, and told them what she'd seen. They said she must have been dreaming, but her father sat with her for a few hours before she was able to fall back asleep.

The next night, Theresa was afraid to go to sleep, so she went in her parents' room and slept in between them. She saw the bright ball again when it came in through the window. This time the lady appeared at the side of the bed. Theresa started shaking her father, but he didn't wake up. She was scared and in awe at the same time.

Mary spoke, telling Theresa, "Don't be afraid." Then she became a ball of light again and disappeared.

All Theresa could talk about the next morning was the lady she'd seen. By now, her mother was convinced that Theresa wasn't just dreaming. She told her daughter that the lady she was describing was the Blessed Mother.

Needless to say, Theresa has always had a great affinity with, and love for, Mary and regularly prays to her. She has told many people her story over the years. Some say she was dreaming and others look at her like she's crazy, but it doesn't really matter. She feels grateful and blessed to have had such a wonderful visit.

In the following story, the vision of Mother Mary was even captured in a photograph:

In 2004, **Rheta Conley**'s father, who had endured a six-month battle with lung, brain, and spinal cancer, was close to passing. He was at his sister's home, comatose, and his family had gathered around.

Sometime during the evening, Rheta and her sister walked into the room where he was, and Rheta exclaimed, "There's a nun at the head of Dad's bed!"

Rheta took a picture with her digital camera, and when she and her sister looked at it, they agreed that it was an image of Mother Mary. This miraculous experience gave everyone in the family comfort during their difficult time.

Digital photography has increased the ability of cameras to capture subtle energies, and almost daily I am shown photos of "orbs of light," which many believe signify the presence of angels. If you go to YouTube and search for videos of Mother Mary or Marian sightings, you'll find numerous examples.

Many of the Marian visions occur when people are in a medical-trauma condition, or are having a near-death experience. While skeptics want to write these events off as stemming from low brain-oxygen levels or hallucinations arising from pain medication, there's no doubt that the visions bring great comfort during highly stressful moments.

Niki Tucci-Delmonico was in a horseback-riding accident on a small island in Greece when she was a teenager (back in the 1990s). She'd been riding since she was 4, and at 15, was quite accomplished. Horses, however, have a mind of their own. Niki fell off a horse one day and broke her ribs, which in turn ruptured her spleen. Unaware of the extent of her injuries, she stayed in a hotel resting for two days. But she got weaker by the hour, so her mother took her to a small clinic on the island, where they did a sonogram to find that she was bleeding internally.

The doctors told her she needed surgery right away, so she and her mother drove to the nearest hospital, which was a few hours away. The whole way there, she really felt no pain and was surprisingly calm.

When they arrived at the hospital, it was as if God had put an angel on their path. There was a Greek doctor there who had trained in Chicago and spoke English. He told Niki that if she had been in the car another five minutes, she would have died. As she was getting prepped for surgery, she was put in a wheelchair in the hallway.

Suddenly, she saw a bright light—so bright that it was as if she were outside in the sunshine—with lots of trees. It felt warm and breezy. And then the Virgin Mary appeared a few feet in front of Niki! She was wearing a white flowing gown and a veil. She had her hands down at her sides, palms up, and her head was tilted. But she wouldn't make eye contact with Niki, as if she were saying, "Go back. It's not your time."

Mother Mary's presence was beautiful, magical, and mystifying—pure heaven! Niki was at peace, experienced no pain, and felt that she was being watched over. She remembers feeling as if she'd been jolted back into her body.

The surgery went amazingly well, and within two weeks, Niki was back to normal. Her belief was always there, but now she has even more of a special bond with Mother Mary and the angels. She is so thankful for the gift of a beautiful life.

৩৩

The light that Niki saw is a common denominator among people having visions of Mother Mary, who glows with radiant Divine love. In Niki's case, the Divine light and love healed her, and reassured her that she still had more living to do.

In the next story, the lights from Mother Mary took a different form:

A number of years ago, **Nanine Locke** and her boyfriend, whom I'll call Steve, were at his apartment after going out to dinner at a beautiful Japanese restaurant, and she felt that something was in the air.

They were standing in his kitchen having a glass of wine, and Steve seemed nervous. Finally, after two hours, he took her hand and asked, "Nanine, will you marry me?"

She was stunned, but excited, too, and she immediately said yes. Steve's roommate came home, but they weren't ready to tell anyone their news yet, so they went into Steve's bedroom and sat on his bed.

The two were excitedly discussing their future, their wedding, and the date, when suddenly Nanine saw little points of light form on Steve's bedroom door. The light seemed to have an energy to it, and then . . . it formed into Mother Mary. She had a shawl over her head and shoulders, and looked very beautiful and loving. The whole time Nanine was looking at her, the points of energy were moving, but still staying in the shape of Mary.

Nanine looked toward the window to make sure no light was entering through there, but none was. She asked her fiancé if he saw what she did, and he said yes.

She asked, "What does it look like to you?" and he replied, "Mary." Her image was there for about ten seconds; then it was gone.

Nanine has always wondered if Mary appeared to them because of all the emotion in the room. But whatever the reason, it set her off on a path of spiritual exploration that has affected her life in positive ways since that day.

The vision of light that Nanine and Steve shared undoubtedly bonded them spiritually as they moved forward into married life. Visions of Mother Mary are healing and transformative, as **Fernando Diaz** recounts:

Fernando was visited twice by Mother Mary. He recalls that she had the most amazingly cuddly energy, just like a supremely loving mother. The most remarkable visitation was on a night when he was in meditation and suddenly opened his eyes to see that Mary was in his room. It was so amazing—she was emanating the most calming and intense blue light.

Mother Mary then showed Fernando how to enter a new reality of his choosing. She was in a bubble-like sphere; then she held another bubble near his heart and told him to place his intentions and dreams in it. She said that when he was ready, he should lift it up and pull it toward him, merging into it so that he and the bubble of his dreams became one. Fernando felt so secure and safe whenever he was in Mary's presence!

The other time Mary appeared to Fernando, he was crying, feeling unsure about his mission on planet Earth. Suddenly, a pink light appeared to him, and he felt Mary's presence at the same time he noticed two angels—one at his right, and one at his left. They started to caress his hair, and he could actually feel the hair moving. Mother Mary then talked to him about his feelings, and he continued crying as she was clearing his energy. But at the same time, he felt so cared for and happy.

Fernando's tears transformed into ones of joy, as he basked in Mary's loving, healing energy. It was an amazing feeling he will never forget!

❧

I find that those who have visions of Mother Mary are people who *believe this is possible.* Their belief allows them to notice and trust images occurring in their minds. If you don't believe it's possible or right to have a vision, then you'll ignore or distrust it when it happens.

Apostle Paul wrote eloquently to the Corinthians that we all possess equal spiritual gifts, and we must use these gifts in the service of love. You've likely had visions yourself. They aren't often three-dimensional or opaque, like seeing a solid human standing before you. Usually, they're fleeting or transparent pictures in your mind's eye, accompanied by insightful thoughts and peaceful feelings.

Dreams of Mary

Many visions of Mother Mary occur within dream time. When you're falling asleep or are fully asleep, your mind is wide open to heavenly visitations. Many people report having powerfully realistic dreams with angels, departed loved ones, Jesus, and Mother Mary. They clearly remember these dreams years later. In a study, psychiatrist and researcher Ian Stevenson distinguished the difference between true visitations and mere dreams. Dr. Stevenson found that true visitations were characterized by strong emotions, a more-than-real feeling, and intense colors. Those who had true visitations also reported that the experience was highly memorable to the point where they could recall details years later.

Dream visitations with Mother Mary happen to people of all walks of life, including nonbelievers. Perhaps those are the ones who most need the connection with the Queen of Angels, as **Walter Mason** discovered:

Walter grew up a good Protestant boy in rural Australia, so he was never exposed to the devotion to Mary. He did, however, have Catholic cousins, and he was drawn to the images of the Virgin that they received for First Communion. He knew they meant something to him, but he didn't know what.

Walter was a bookseller for many years, and regularly attended the massive trade fairs that fill convention halls all over the world. He was working through a particularly exhausting and stressful cycle of fairs, feeling tired of his job and his life. He had lost all hope for himself and his future.

One night he went to bed footsore and spiritually exhausted. He slept deeply, and had the most remarkable dream. He was walking through an enormous trade fair, packed with people, yet he was incapable of moving forward or back. He was angry and tired and wanted to escape. Then he felt someone tap his shoulder and, spinning around in annoyance, was shocked to discover the Blessed Virgin standing directly behind him with a look of the purest but most profound compassion on her face.

"You don't realize it," she said to Walter, smiling, "but I love you so much, and I always will."

Hearing this, he woke up and started crying, with tears of joy more than anything else. Just to recount the story makes him cry, even though he had the dream 15 years ago.

Some years later, Walter was on a journal retreat. It was being held at a mostly empty old nunnery high on a hill in the outer suburbs of Sydney. The first night finished late, and he had arranged for his partner to pick him up, as there was no public transportation to this remote spot. When he came out, the parking lot was empty, and his cell phone had no reception. He was a little annoyed, but he knew that his partner wouldn't have forgotten him. Normally he would have sat on a bench and waited, but an inner voice told him to start walking.

Walter moved down the drive, but he soon got lost in the grounds of this old place, which had once been a dairy farm. There were no lights, no one was around, and he became frightened and disoriented. He was moving down the hill, he knew that, but where would he end up?

Suddenly he saw before him a slightly glowing white figure that was clearly the Virgin Mary. *Well,* he thought, *this is a nunnery—the chances of a statue of the Virgin being somewhere on the grounds are really high.* But this figure grew brighter and brighter and began to move. He trusted it totally, and began to follow. All of his anxiety left him, and he felt almost deliriously happy. He was led through the park and, by a side gate, to the entrance of a small house where some elderly priests lived. Outside this house he found his partner parked, sound asleep in the driver's seat. There had been some confusion about the address, and he had simply gone to the only religious institution he could find in the area. His phone, too, had no reception. They would have both been waiting for hours if Walter hadn't been guided by Mother Mary!

Walter's dream visitation helped him feel connected to Mother Mary, and allowed him to have the clear vision afterward. The powerful love she expressed to him allowed him to trust her maternal guidance, which led him where he needed to go.

Mary watches over the planet and all of its inhabitants. Not only does she enter dreams to help us personally, but she also gives us prophetic dreams related to world situations:

The night before the devastating 2011 earthquake and tsunami in Japan, **Christina Wedebrook** had a dream. In it, she and her husband and daughter were traveling down a road, and on both sides were gravestones. Christina insisted that they stop at the cemetery. When she got out of the car, she walked into the middle of the plots and looked up into the beautiful blue sky, which was filled with white puffy clouds. One of the clouds became the Virgin Mary and floated down to her. Christina took her hand; and Mary fell to the ground, sobbing uncontrollably.

Christina had prophetic dreams quite often, so when she woke up the next morning and learned of the natural disaster, she immediately knew why Mary was crying so sorrowfully in her dream, as the Blessed Mother sheds tears for all those who are suffering and in pain.

Those who have prophetic dreams about tragedies often wonder why they're given this information. They worry, *Since I foresaw the event, could I have done something to prevent it?* My experience has taught me that you would have been given specific instructions if you were supposed to intervene. In the absence of clear guidance to take action, though, prophetic dreams are a call for you to pray for peace, protection, and healing, as Christina did.

Although dreams frequently don't make logical sense, they always have underlying messages that we can divine through analysis and doing research. In this way, the dream's message becomes understandable and clear. Mother Mary's prophetic dream visitations can also include news of significant current events:

Usually, **Ros Booth**'s connections with Mother Mary started with a dream. But when she woke up on one particular morning, she remembered one of the most intense dream visitations she'd ever had in her life. She recalled being in a large building and joining a group in an old-fashioned kitchen. She then found herself in an adjacent room, where there was a poster bed with a crisscross design. The room then widened, and she could see a mantel with a statue of Mother Mary above the fireplace, and a wooden chair. She knew instinctively that Saint Bernadette had passed away there, and she could feel her presence.

When she awoke, the images were still very vivid, but she really had no idea who this Saint Bernadette was, other than childhood memories of a black-and-white movie.

Ros wasn't Catholic, but she had started visiting a grotto for prayer healing, so she was prompted to ask a Catholic friend, "Who is Saint Bernadette?"

Ros's friend gave her a children's scripture book, and Ros also did some Internet research. She read that young Bernadette had become a nun after having visions of Mother Mary, and despite being ridiculed, she maintained her faith. The area where Bernadette had her visions is now the famous Lourdes commune in France.

Ros gasped in shock when she found photographs of the room, exactly as she had envisioned, where Saint Bernadette had indeed lived and passed away.

Throughout this wonderful visitation, Saint Bernadette introduced Ros to Mother Mary more fully. Ros continued to visit the healing grotto, and often felt the presence of Mary and her son, Jesus. Occasionally, she would know Mary was present by the faint wafting perfume of roses. Her energy was soft, gentle, and subtle.

However, it was not long before Ros would need the healing comfort of Mother Mary to mend her own grieving heart. A close friend who was Catholic had passed away unexpectedly of cancer, so Ros was invited to attend a special mass in her memory at a reception hall. During this time of quiet reflection, Ros could feel a presence standing next to her. Rose-scented perfume filled her senses, and as she breathed in this welcoming aroma, Ros could feel peace wash over her.

Although she was sad and tearful, Ros truly felt that she was not alone. She mentally thanked Mary and could feel her standing closer to her. She sat and cried, missing her friend, but was heartened that Mother Mary continued to surround her with love and comfort. Ros could see her presence as a slight haze.

At the funeral the next day, Ros felt Mother Mary's presence supporting everyone in the room. As gentle as a soft hand on a shoulder—kind and compassionate—Mary helped shift the heaviness of grief to a lightness of spirit.

Over time, Ros has asked for Mary's help in surrounding and comforting others, as the Beloved Mother did for her. She loves the fact that Mother Mary came into her life through Saint Bernadette, who spent her life in service after visions of Our Lady prompted her to trust her faith. That same year, Ros's own personal journey of service led her to be certified as an Angel Intuitive™. She has learned to trust her clairvoyant visions as she provides healing and guidance for others.

She is so very grateful for Mother Mary's loving support.

Having corroborated the details of Saint Bernadette's passing through doing post-dream research, Ros found that her trust in Mother Mary increased. Mother Mary also comes into our dreams when our loved ones pass away, to reassure and comfort us. These dreams can heal a grieving heart, as **Lisa Moreau** discovered:

When Lisa was in college, her grandmother Agnes passed away. People often embellish the character of those who have died, but in Agnes's case, the accolades were true: she really was an angel! She projected pure, unconditional love, and Lisa felt honored to have even been related to her.

Because she was so very close to her grandmother and loved her so deeply, her death was difficult for Lisa on many levels: it was her first experience with losing a loved one, she wasn't able to be with her when she died, she couldn't attend her funeral because of the distance, and she never got to tell her good-bye.

For months after her grandmother's death, Lisa continued to grieve terribly, constantly torturing herself by thinking, *I didn't even get to say good-bye.* Then one night, she had a dream, which she knows was much more than a dream; it just felt so real.

In it, Lisa was with her grandmother in what felt like her house. It was a very plain room with a wooden floor, one window, and nothing there except for a statue of Mother Mary. Lisa looked out the window and saw clouds, so she felt that she and Agnes were in heaven. The two spoke with their hearts and minds. They embraced, and Lisa felt pure love and light surge between them.

Agnes then motioned toward the statue of Mary, whose alabaster face was glowing with love, with her light blue cloak flowing to her feet.

Even though this all happened 25 years ago, Lisa still remembers the image of the statue clearly. Her grandmother told her—through thought—that Mother Mary was the one who had brought them together . . . that she had made the meeting possible.

Growing up in a strong Catholic family, Lisa had always felt connected to Mother Mary, but she felt especially grateful to her at that moment. After the dream, or rather, *experience,* Lisa never tortured herself again with grief over her grandmother. She still cried, and still missed her greatly, but it wasn't the same type of sorrow any longer. She felt lighter and freer after the experience, and she thanks Mother Mary for giving her a chance to tell her grandmother good-bye and hug her one last time.

Lisa's dream of the Mother Mary statue coming to life is a common theme for many who see the Blessed Mother in their dreams and visions. Like Lisa, **Julie Miller** had a dream in which Mother Mary appeared unexpectedly and helped her heal from grief:

Julie had a childhood friend named Marilynn who had died in 1978 at the age of 19. She had hit her head at work, and then strangely and suddenly died of an aneurism. It was very shocking. Although the two girls had grown apart and really hadn't kept in touch after Julie went to college, she was quite disturbed and saddened by Marilynn's death.

Marilynn would come to Julie in dreams many times. She didn't remember what her friend said to her exactly, but she got the feeling that it was something like "I'm okay." Now, dreaming about loved ones who had crossed over wasn't that unusual for Julie, as she often had these types of dreams. But she had one particular dream about Marilynn that was really memorable. She actually remembered it clearly, and it was symbolic, literally.

Marilynn was standing at the window in this dream. She didn't say anything to Julie, but she wanted her to follow her and look at her. Marilynn was showing her the light from the window. Julie kept watching and looking, and finally an object that resembled a clear CD case appeared in the air out of the light in the window. She followed it in curious wonderment, thinking, *What is that?*

It began to roll forward, tumbling toward her. Julie was a little scared, but she was totally mesmerized by this thing. It was getting bigger and bigger, and a geometric-like shape was revealed. She no longer saw Marilynn, only the light that was beginning to emanate from this shape as it came closer to her. It exploded in color, and this unbelievable light transformed into Mother Mary. Julie remembers just bathing in this radiant light.

She awoke in disbelief, shock, and awe, saying things like: "What does this mean?" and "Oh my God, that was so incredible!" She couldn't stop thinking about it.

To this day, Julie feels so blessed to know how wonderful, loving, gentle, and powerful Mother Mary's message of love is for us. If she had to recall the message of the Blessed Mother's appearance, she thinks the word *connection* would come up. That is, Mary doesn't want us to lose our connection with each other.

Mother Mary reminds us that we are all brothers and sisters, even if we were estranged at the time of death, like Julie and Marilynn. The compassion of Mother Mary helps us relax like a trusting child and open our hearts to her outpouring of healing love. She nurtures our souls back to health.

In the next chapter, we'll explore how Mother Mary also heals our physical bodies in miraculous ways.

CHAPTER TWO

MOTHER MARY PHYSICAL HEALINGS

Healings arising from Mother Mary visitations, apparitions, and prayers have been reported for centuries. Sixty-seven miracle healings from Lourdes have been studied, investigated, and validated by the Lourdes Medical Bureau and the Catholic Church. Researchers believe that there are at least 5,000 that haven't yet been validated, but are nonetheless credible. The Lourdes Medical Bureau substantiates the person's diagnosis and the cure, and calls it an "inexplicable healing" when a miracle is the only explanation for the person's return to wellness.

Many of the healings described in this chapter came in people's darkest hour, when they were on their knees needing help. I've found that this complete surrender often precedes a miracle healing. Our surrender isn't an egoic requirement of heaven. Rather, it means we're getting out of the way so that heaven can intervene.

For example, after **Betty McWilliam** was diagnosed with breast cancer, she quickly had two surgeries, and then her oncologist started her on a course of radical chemotherapy. Her body couldn't handle the harsh drugs, and she was hospitalized on many occasions following each treatment.

She had never felt sick with the cancer, but the treatments were debilitating to her body. She was given an infusion of four drugs, which took five to seven hours to complete, every three weeks. Within a few days of treatment, she would get extremely sick—similar to, but much worse than, food poisoning (which she had experienced many years earlier).

Betty wasn't at all afraid to leave the planet and go to her Lord, but when she asked if it was her time to go, she got the message: *Not yet.* After each treatment, she would feel herself moving out into her auric field. She would become weaker and weaker, and start floating above her body. She simply didn't know how to stay here and survive the treatments, so she prayed to Mother Mary, Jesus, and Archangel Raphael (the angel of healing) each day—and sometimes *many* times a day.

Then, after her third treatment, she couldn't keep any food down and kept passing out. Her husband took her to the hospital one more time. She no longer cared what happened to her body, as she was too weak and exhausted to carry on. Her oncologist determined that she had a bleeding ulcer and sent her to another hospital for emergency surgery. She phoned her sons to tell them what was happening so they wouldn't worry, but by the time she was registered at the other hospital, they had arrived to help her husband keep vigil.

During the night, Betty looked over at her sons' faces and saw the pain and fear in their eyes. She saw the same thing on her exhausted husband's face. How could she get through this for them? she wondered.

Again, she prayed to Mother Mary to help her. As she lay there, she could feel two gentle hands holding her face. She looked up to see which of her sons it was, because the hands were too small to be her husband's. Instead, she saw Mother Mary, wearing her white veil, smiling down at her. Betty then knew that the Blessed Mother would take care of her until she had her surgery the next day, and that all would be well.

She continued to pray to Mother Mary to guide her doctors in any further treatments. When she went back to her oncologist a week later, he decided that he would take her off three of the four drugs because her body was just too sensitive to continue the harsh chemo treatments. Her prayers had been answered. She stayed on the one remaining drug until June of that year, and her doctor told her in July that she was cancer free. She always knew that she no longer had cancer, but it took Mother Mary to convince the doctors to phase out the treatments.

Betty continues to ask Mother Mary to care for her sons, grandchildren, and daughters-in-law, who will soon be giving her two more grandchildren. She and her husband know that they are very blessed to have such a loving family, and she is certain that Mother Mary helped her stay here on Earth to give those children the love they need to flourish in this world. Each of them has a special gift to offer to humankind, and Betty is sure that Mother Mary will guide them, as she guides and continues to help *her*.

The absolute faith that Betty held, plus her fervent prayers, allowed room for Divine intervention. All of heaven respects our free will and won't intrude upon our choices, awaiting our invitation to intervene, and then our surrender to Divine will.

Like Betty, **Tina Ferraro** received Divine guidance that it wasn't her time to go yet, despite her doctors' grim prognoses. Tina had a dream of Mother Mary that involved a statue coming to life, something I mentioned earlier as a common theme among Mary visitations. I believe that these visitations and dreams gave both Betty and Tina the courage and strength to fight for their lives.

Back in early 2005, Tina, who was 33 at the time, woke up in the early hours of the morning with a vision of Mother Mary and Jesus. She often saw Jesus in her dreams, and he would watch over her, smile at her, and talk to her. He was like a best friend, and it felt very comfortable.

This time, he stood in the background behind Mother Mary while she spoke. It was the first time Tina had ever seen her. She remembers sitting on the edge of her bed smiling back at the Blessed Mother, who was beaming the whole time. Tina really couldn't remember the entire conversation, but she was left with the feeling that she would have a big battle ahead, but all would be well.

About a month later, Tina was diagnosed with a rare lung condition and was told that without a double lung transplant, she would have maybe six months to live. She recalls that when the doctors gave her the diagnosis, she confidently told them that she wasn't going anywhere, and that it would be okay. Of course, they thought she was crazy and in denial.

But five years passed, and Mother Mary, in the form of a statue, appeared to Tina once more in a dream. But when Tina looked at her, Mary moved—that is, the statue came to life.

Tina fell to her knees and prayed, and as it happened, that day she ended up in the hospital due to her condition, which had weakened her heart. The doctors tried a drug that she really didn't want to take after reading about its many negative side effects, and as a result, Tina almost lost the fight for her life.

But she survived, so she realized that there were bigger plans than she could ever imagine in store for her.

Tina now believes that her two visions of Mother Mary occurred to let her know that she is being watched over, and she finds great comfort in that knowledge. She also knows that the Blessed Mother will appear to her again in her dreams whenever she needs her assistance.

I join Tina in believing that visions and dreams of Mother Mary are her way of letting us know that she's right here, next to all of us, as a lovingly watchful parent. Sometimes, a person doesn't even need a spiritual vision of Mother Mary to effect a healing. In this next story, a picture was enough to elicit a miracle:

Patricia Acosta Ruiz grew up as a Catholic and has always had a connection with Mother Mary, who was a very nurturing energy in her life. Once, when she was 12 years old, her aunt Maureen (from her father's side) was very ill in the hospital. Everyone gathered around her and assumed she was "at death's door." She had cancer of the lungs, was having great difficulty breathing, and was in the ICU. Patricia had in her possession a very old and tattered picture of "Our Lady of Perpetual Succor," and felt intuitively that she had to give it to her aunt and somehow place it under her pillow so that she could be helped by Mother Mary.

Patricia's uncle Robert was a self-proclaimed atheist, but being very emotional and sad about his wife, he told Patricia that he would try anything to help his wife. Following his niece's instructions, he took the card and placed it under Maureen's pillow. Within days, she started getting better, and the cancer went into remission. She lived another two years.

Robert told Patricia how grateful he was, and that he was convinced that it was Mother Mary who had helped his wife. He said it was truly the first bit of proof for him that God actually exists.

Miracle healings have a way of creating believers. When there's no other explanation except Divine intervention, everyone takes note. I believe that Mother Mary wants us to know that she's with us and that she brings God's love to heal us, especially during desperate times. Just like any loving mother, she wants us to have faith, to feel safe, and to enjoy good health. Mother Mary also acts quickly during emergency situations, as **Denise Drapikowski** experienced with her husband:

This loving story of the Blessed Mother will stay with Denise for the rest of her life. She retells it often to family members, as she treasures the wonderful way in which Mary has connected with her.

Denise and her dear husband, Bob, were having a loving day together in May a few years ago. They had just taken a casual walk along a lovely spring-garden area lining their riverfront town. Since it was Mother's Day, they decided to go home a little bit early so that they could spend more time with their college-age daughter. As they proceeded to their car and turned on the engine, it suddenly started to sputter and backfire, and smoke poured out of the engine. They both jumped out of the car.

Bob opened the hood and flames shot out. He shouted for Denise to move away and dial 911. He started to run back and forth, pouring dirt and sand on top of the engine, hoping to extinguish the flames.

In a matter of ten minutes or less, the fire company had arrived and doused the flames. Suddenly, Bob fell to the ground, unconscious. The ambulance team, thankfully, was on the scene and started CPR.

By this time near to hysteria, Denise started praying to Our Dear Lady: "Please, Blessed Mother, don't let Bob die on Mother's Day." The medics continued to use the life-support defibrillator on her husband and rushed him to the emergency room. Denise could only stand there in shock with the police and her close relatives, who had arrived to take her and her daughter to the hospital. She remembers that she had a Miraculous Medal (an item of devotion in Catholicism believed to bring special graces through the intercession of Mary) in her pocket. She asked Mother Mary to be "Miraculous" for Bob and keep him alive.

She was squeezing the medal so hard while praying that she had an indent in her palm when she arrived at the ER, nearly half an hour later. Denise and her daughter still didn't know what Bob's condition was or even if he was still alive. They stood around for about five minutes, and then the doctor came over to them, put his arm around Denise's shoulders, and said, "I am truly amazed. I've never seen such a fast and miraculous recovery in someone who had clearly flatlined."

When Denise and her daughter went in to see Bob, he was sitting up, asking for them.

Denise truly believes that Our Lady showed her miraculous powers on that Mother's Day.

(Denise and her husband had three more wonderful years together, until he did pass on from complications of heart surgery in March of 2006.)

Sometimes, Mother Mary's miracle healings occur without medical intervention or corroboration, as in a woman named **Fay**'s case. Although no doctors were involved in her situation, Fay knows that her Mother Mary visitation was lifesaving:

Fay was at her friend's wedding. It had been a really hot day, and she was starting to develop a bad headache. She and her then boyfriend went home, and she got into bed. She'd been getting terrible migraines, which would start with impaired vision, and then half an hour later she would be sick, with a throbbing ache like a band over her head for at least two days.

But this headache was very different. There had been no warning sign of impaired vision, and the pain was very sharp and intense in a single area, like someone driving a spear in. It got so bad that even though Fay is someone who doesn't like to cause a fuss, she realized that something was very wrong and asked her boyfriend to call an ambulance. Unfortunately, he didn't believe it was that bad and went downstairs. He worked in a hospital, so she figured he was used to seeing people who were much more ill.

At this point, the pain was beyond excruciating. Fay was so sick that she couldn't even move. Although at the time she didn't really know about angels and wasn't religious, she called out to God to please help her. It occurred to her that she really might die, and there was a sense of peace connected to this realization. Although Fay was young, she'd experienced a lot of difficult things in her life. It wasn't that she *wanted* to die; it was just that it all felt like too much, and she couldn't bear the physical pain any longer.

Suddenly, a loud mechanical noise started grinding from outside the window, like nothing Fay had ever heard. That side of the house just faced the next house; there weren't even any trees. It sounded like heavy machinery was getting louder and closer to the window near her head, and she was really scared. Then a few feet from her bed, two lights appeared, whizzing around each other in a spiraling cone shape from the floor to about five feet in height. Within this, a figure of shimmering gold light began to appear. It looked just like Mother Mary, who was wearing a long robe and a headdress.

Being a practical person, Fay assumed she was hallucinating, but every time she looked, Mary was still there. So she decided to test herself. She sat up straight, rubbed her eyes, and then opened them. Mary was still there—so close and so real! It was the most fantastic thing she'd ever seen. She cried out for her boyfriend to come and see this most amazing thing, but just as he came in, Mary vanished. The pain had vanished, too, and Fay was completely healed.

Fay believes she had a stroke, rather than a migraine, that night, and that if it hadn't been for Mother Mary, she would have died. But the Blessed Mother obviously had other plans for Fay, and whenever she thinks of her shining image, it reminds her to have faith in herself and her life purpose, for which she is very grateful.

Even though her boyfriend didn't witness Mother Mary's visitation or believe that she was seriously ill, Fay knew the truth. Her faith increased because of her experience, just as it did for many others who have told me about their Mother Mary encounters and healings. In fact, this next story shows how Mother Mary helps and heals people of all different faiths:

Ani Moonsamy underwent a major operation on her uterus and urethra in June of 2000. As a result, her post-op recovery was extremely slow and difficult. Most of her days were spent in deep depression, pain, frustration, and constant tears. She couldn't even move without assistance. Ani also found that it was very difficult for her to sleep at night, as she was dosing herself with painkillers during the day and slept during those hours, so at night she was restless.

Although a Hindu by religion, she has always considered herself a child of the universe, so she loves and respects all religions—her belief is that we are all *one*.

Anyway, one night at around 10 P.M., Ani again struggled to fall asleep. Her husband was watching television in the TV room while she remained in her bed with the lights switched off, and she finally fell asleep, awash in tears. Within minutes, she felt a calm, bright white light over her bed, hovering above her body. There was so much love and warmth that she felt herself smile through her tears!

The light enveloped Ani so comfortingly that she succumbed freely to it. Its warmth moved gently through her entire body, through the area that was operated upon, and gradually out her feet, leaving them feeling warm and toasty! Only at that moment did Ani slowly open her eyes. There in front of her, at her feet, was Mother Mary! So splendidly in the pure white light did she stand—and with so much love that it penetrated Ani's soul!

Ani found herself sitting up gently, trying to move toward Mary, and then she sat watching in total amazement. Slowly, as if to say that her work on her was complete, Mary "disappeared" through the opening in her bedroom closet. Thinking that it was her imagination, Ani was nevertheless so mesmerized that she unknowingly stood up and found herself switching on her bedroom lights to see where Mary had gone.

Ani's screams of amazement brought her husband running into her bedroom, and when he saw her standing on her own, he couldn't believe his eyes. Previously he'd had to help her get out of bed! He sat her down as she told him what had occurred, and he too admitted that the room felt so "blessed and peaceful."

From that night on, Ani's recovery was rapid, and she soon returned to work. When she related her experience to a close colleague, Ani expressed that she wanted to get an image of Mother Mary to place in her shrine. One morning when Ani got to work, there was a small gift box left on her desk. When she opened it, she found the most beautiful statue of Mother Mary (which looked very similar to the blessed being who had visited her!).

Ani's colleague said that she had been so moved when Ani told her about her experience that she went to a monastery and inquired about the statue. Of course, Ani's appreciation was boundless; and she realized that not only had her body been healed spiritually, mentally, physically, and emotionally, but her soul had been eternally blessed!

Those who have had an encounter with Mother Mary feel deep gratitude and appreciation, and a strong connection with her. Like a nurturing parent, the Divine Mother responds instantly to our cries for help. She'll do anything possible to ensure that our prayers are answered, as **Roberta Romanoski** discovered:

Roberta's 81-year-old father was very ill. The doctor called one morning and said that her dad would not live beyond that day, so she and her mother went to the nursing facility and stayed with him. He began to have terrible pain, but the nurses said that they couldn't authorize giving him an injection, only the doctor could, and he wasn't in attendance that night.

Roberta went to another room and said a prayer to Mother Mary. She asked Mary to talk to her son, Jesus, to see if he could help her father. She explained that the pain her father was experiencing was terrible, and that it was not helping him in any way. She added that human beings have a limit as to what they can endure. Roberta thanked Mary for listening and returned to see her dad. About 20 minutes later, the doctor walked into the room, saw the condition that Roberta's dad was in, and said that there was no reason for him to have to experience that. He administered the painkiller shot.

Almost instantly, Roberta's father ceased to feel any pain. He passed away later that night at peace and with a beautiful smile on his face. Roberta's mom said he looked like a baby, and that all the wrinkles on his face had disappeared.

The doctor, who was wearing a tuxedo, told Roberta that he had been driving to a dinner party when all of a sudden he felt compelled to go to the nursing facility and see her father. He had no idea why this thought had come to his mind. He tried to ignore it and continue on to the dinner party, but his car refused to travel in that direction. The steering wheel would only turn in the direction of the nursing facility!

Roberta realized that the thought had come to the doctor's mind within a few minutes of her appeal to Mother Mary. She and her son, Jesus, surely were fast workers, and Roberta and her mom were so very grateful!

Although Roberta's father passed away, Mother Mary and Jesus's compassionate help was still in evidence. Roberta and her family felt much better, knowing that her father went to heaven peacefully. The synchronistic timing of the doctor's visit, prompted by his intuition, confirmed that her prayers were heard and answered.

Prayers are *always* heard and answered, but often in unexpected ways. Mother Mary, like all nurturing and wise parents, wants her children to be safe and happy. So when we ask for peace, security, health, and such, she will lead us there even if the pathway differs from our expectations.

Mother Mary supports our wellness by guiding us to take excellent care of our bodies. She gently leads us to eat healthfully, exercise, get sufficient sleep, and detoxify. And in a woman named **Linda**'s case, Mother Mary even helped her join a fitness center:

After losing the life she knew and being thrown into a living nightmare, Linda was slowly starting to wake up and see the light, but she still felt numb and nearly dead inside. Throughout her struggles, she was constantly encountering signs that she wasn't alone, but due to her emotional state, she would usually credit her imagination for the support. That is, until Mother Mary removed all doubt.

Because of physical and emotional injuries, Linda nearly doubled her weight, a key factor in preventing her from progressing in her recovery. But she couldn't afford what she most wanted to help her regain her health and confidence: a gym membership. One night, Linda cried herself to sleep, thinking about how much she wanted the gym membership so she could feel like herself again; but above all, she wished she could get a clear sign that she really hadn't been abandoned by God and the angelic realm.

The next morning, Linda woke up with the persistent thought of selling her jewelry, so she went to an indoor swap meet with many little jewelry stands in order to do so. Linda was then drawn to a tiny stand in what felt like the middle of nowhere.

She asked the man behind the counter if he was interested in buying jewelry, and as she was talking to him, she felt the need to look in the display case, where she saw a beautiful Mother Mary medallion. Linda was in such desperation that she prayed to her for the first time in years. She asked Mary to please help her not only sell her jewelry, but also get enough money to buy a gym membership. After examining Linda's jewelry, the man told her he would give her the best price anywhere per ounce. He calculated the total, and when he read it to her, her eyes immediately teared up—it was almost the exact amount of money that she needed. Linda naturally accepted the man's offer and immediately went to buy her gym membership.

At the end of the day, she ended up with the gym membership she so desperately wanted; one more penny in her wallet (what was left from the jewelry sale); and best of all, a warm, happy feeling in her heart.

Ever since then, whenever Linda has needed an extra push, Mother Mary always finds a way to put in an appearance just to make her smile and help her keep going.

Like a concerned parent, Mother Mary wants you to take good care of your physical health. So she will guide and arrange for you to exercise, just as she did for Linda. She'll also help you develop an improved lifestyle, including reducing or eliminating unhealthful cravings.

For example, **Pat Klebes** had tried to quit smoking for ten years. She'd bought all types of programs and gadgets, but was still smoking two packs a day, just like she had been doing for 40-plus years.

Her doctor suggested that she go on the nicotine patch for a full three months, rather than just the six weeks recommended by the manufacturer. So, every morning Pat would put on her Miraculous Medal, say a Hail Mary, and pray to the Blessed Mother that she please be given the strength to not smoke, and also to remove any thoughts or desires about cigarette smoking from her mind. Pat was also saying a no-vena (a nine-day prayer) to the Miraculous Medal.

After two weeks, she was coming home from work and realized that she was out of patches and didn't have enough money to buy more, and she didn't want to charge them to her credit card. So she said, "Well, Mother Mary, tomorrow we're on our own." The next morning, she put on her medal, said the Hail Mary, and again made her prayer request.

Well, to her surprise, she has never had a craving for a cigarette since that day—an absolute miracle. Pat has been cigarette-free for 12 years now, but she still says the Hail Mary and prays to the Blessed Mother every day!

Any loving parent would want her children to be imme-diately comforted, so Mother Mary's healings are often in-stantaneous. When **Maya Bringas** asked Mary to heal away her pain, her prayer was immediately answered:

Maya has had several experiences with Mother Mary that touched her. For instance, many years ago, when she was about 20, she woke up with severe pains in her lower abdomen. It was like nothing she'd ever experienced before; she was in agony. Since it was the middle of the night, she didn't want to get up and disturb her parents, so she stayed in bed.

At that time, Maya kept a small statue of Mother Mary on her bedside table, so she touched the statue, asking for the pain to go away. She then started to place her hands in various positions on her abdominal area. After just a few minutes, the pain completely disappeared! She was then able to fall back to sleep.

The next morning, Maya told her parents what had hap-pened, and also went to the doctor to check things out, even though she had no discomfort. The doctor explained that it was menstrual cramps, something Maya had never experienced before the previous night, which is why she was so confused about what was happening to her body.

That day Maya bought some carnations and placed them on her altar at home as an offering to Mother Mary to thank her for healing her pain. It truly was a miracle, and she was so grateful to the Blessed Mother! It's been about 15 or so years since that night, and she has never experienced cramps like that again. She knows that Mother Mary is always with her, protecting and guiding her.

Maya's healing is another illustration of Mother Mary's sweet and gentle support. She nurtures us physically *and* emotionally so that we may enjoy our lives, as we'll explore in the next chapter.

CHAPTER THREE

MOTHER MARY EMOTIONAL HEALINGS

Not only does Mother Mary support and guide our physical health, but she also intervenes when our emotions need healing and uplifting. The Beloved Mother heals our hearts, because she knows that our emotional well-being affects every other area of our lives.

For example, **Karen McGregor** was sitting on her bed holding her precious carving of Mother Mary to her heart as she reflected on the last two years of chaos, crying, and desperation. Despite Karen's best efforts to "hold it all together," she felt that her life was falling apart, as she was not only separating from her husband of 14 years, but she had also lost both of her business partners and had spent the summer in the hospital with her son, who was healing from a broken leg.

It was here that Karen met Mary. Growing up Catholic, she had an idea of who the Blessed Mother was based on scriptures and homilies, but she had never had the actual *experience* of Mary. That is, she had never had the heart-based connection to her as a Divine Feminine essence. Her understanding was mind-based, rather than something that penetrated the edges of her spiritual core.

Karen had not known true desperation until that summer. While in this agitated state, she saw images of Mary in her mind and felt her warmth in her heart. She began to pray, discovering what unconditional love felt like in her body. She continued to reach out to the Blessed Mother, because something deep within her wanted her help—help to leave Earth, if only for a while, and be with her, wherever that was. Karen threw herself, arms and legs splayed, onto her bed, begging to be released from the nightmare she had created.

However, Karen really didn't expect anything to change, so she pleaded with God: "Please just take me; this is too hard. I don't want to be here anymore." Through her sobs, through her bodily breakdown, Karen heard Mary's voice say, "Focus on your heart." As she did so, her heart warmed, which was followed by an intense heat that within minutes felt like a burning fire. She continued, with surprising calm, to focus on her heart and was soon embraced by the Divine light that some term a "near-death experience." She felt weightless, as if she were part of the air around her, and the warm white light bathed her in love. She did nothing except be a part of this heaven; she did not think, act, or move. She was simply *one* with the universe.

When she returned back to the present, with the gentle direction of Mary, she knew that she had experienced the heart of the Sacred Feminine, the heart of Mary. The very thing she tried to snuff out of existence in an effort to protect herself was her saving grace.

Since that day, Karen's life has shifted in the most profound ways. She has discovered the powerful, infinite heart of Mary within, and her capacity to love and *be* loved. She is also helping others experience the radiant beauty available to them when they open their hearts, and the bliss of a deeper connection with Spirit.

Mary has taught Karen that the pure simplicity of a loving, open heart is the most precious thing there is. Blessed be the Queen of Angels!

Mary is mother to all, a nurturing and protective parent who intervenes to keep us healthy and happy. She knows exactly the remedy for any condition, and has saved many lives through her miraculous love, as the following story illustrates:

Chloée B. has been a practicing Catholic her entire life. During her youth in France, God and the angels were always in her heart. But she didn't think of asking them for their help to overcome the difficulties and suffering she endured.

When she was 20 years old, Chloée fell into a depression, coupled with anorexia, and she was hospitalized in Paris for a long and trying month. She was locked in her room 24 hours a day, without being permitted to have contact with anyone in the outside world. She was also subjected to psychological and physical mistreatment. Her only comfort was being able to go to the hospital chapel in the morning and evening to contemplate a very beautiful statue of the Virgin Mary. During that month, Mary's loving, soft smile helped Choée turn little by little toward God and the angels.

Chloée came to realize that her life was in the hands of an invisible power, and that the earthly life made sense only if she understood it as a gift from God. Her cure was possible, thanks to God, and it was Mary, with her smile, who taught that to her. After the painful experience in the hospital, it was Mary who helped Chloée return to her Catholic faith, and who helped her believe in God's love, even when she was in danger of dying.

Chloée's eating disorders lasted ten years, but without Mother Mary, she wouldn't have survived: her weight had gotten too low, and her heart was affected by her condition. She was aware that she could die at any time, and when things got very bad, she would hold an effigy of the Virgin Mary in her hands and squeeze it. She would pray to her and say that she didn't want to die. Chloée would then hear a loving voice telling her, "Don't worry. You will manage."

One time, Chloée actually felt Mother Mary's hand on her shoulder. She felt the contact on her skin, which both marked her with her love and with Mary's tangible imprint.

A major shift occurred during Chloée's visit to the sanctuary of Pontmain, which is dedicated to Our Lady. Chloée always refused to eat anything other than beans or apples, and her body suffered from severe nutritional deficiencies. She was conscious that it was vital that she adopt better food habits, at least by reintroducing protein into her diet, but she hadn't managed to make this healthful change.

On this day, while at the sanctuary, Chloée asked Mary to help her, and when she left, she suddenly had the desire to eat starches and fish. Since that day, her diet has included these foods, and she is back to her normal weight. She has also started exercising, and has even gone back to work.

Mary helps Chloée every day now, both with her nutritional habits and her practice of Catholicism. She hears a deep, soft voice guiding her in her material and spiritual life. And it is also thanks to Mary that Chloée has embarked on the study of angels.

How miraculous and fortunate that her appetite shifted immediately, allowing her to regain her strength and health. With her better diet and lifestyle, Chloée's emotions and energy levels are now healthy.

Mother Mary heals a heart heavy with grief following a loss. I experienced this personally when I appealed to her for comfort after a close friend's death. I felt her gentle embrace and warm sweet love help my grief-numbed heart reawaken. In the following story, Mother Mary provided similar miraculous aid to a woman who had just lost her mother:

Patricia "Lois" Lance had taken care of her terminally ill mother for nine and a half months before her ultimate death. During that time, a group of five spiritualists, healers, and psychics came into their lives. Lois's mother called these ladies her "Earth angels."

A week after her mom's death, four of these wonderful ladies drove Lois to the airport, as she had to go out of town. Two of them kept telling her, "Mother Mary is with you again today. Her presence is very strong. She is surrounding you with love and light." Lois was traveling from Bellingham, Washington, to Harrisburg, Pennsylvania, via Seattle.

During the flight, Lois closed her eyes and gave heartfelt thanks to God for the wonderful experience of caring for her mother, who had prepared her well for her own death, as she had the remarkable ability to teach without words. All of a sudden, Lois felt a surge of love that enveloped her, much like a huge, warm hug. It was a feeling of peace and calm that she had never experienced before.

When the plane landed in Seattle, she rose to exit. There was a severely crippled, elderly woman trying to make her way down the aisle, and she was struggling with a piece of carry-on luggage. Lois hadn't noticed her when she'd boarded the plane in Bellingham. The stewardess kept saying, "Hurry up, ma'am, hurry up!"

Lois thought the flight attendant was extremely rude to speak to the woman in that tone and not even offer to help her. She tapped the elderly woman on her shoulder and asked her if she could carry her luggage for her. The woman turned to her and said, "Why, thank you, my angel."

When they were at the bottom of the airplane stairs, walking on the tarmac toward the terminal, the woman took her arm and said, "You are so kind to help me. I have rheumatoid arthritis. I walk slowly because my hips hurt. And my hands are so crippled—just look at them. What is your name, dear?"

Lois told her, and the woman said, "I have another plane to catch."

"Well, I have an hour before my plane leaves for Harrisburg," Lois replied. "Let me please carry your luggage and accompany you to your gate." The older woman squeezed Lois's arm and thanked her profusely.

When they were almost to the gate, Lois asked, "By the way, what's your name?"

The woman answered, "My name is Mary."

"What a beautiful name," Lois remarked. "It's so nice to meet you." When they got to the gate, there was a small line at the check-in counter. Lois asked Mary if she would like her to wait with her.

She said, "No, dear. Thank you so much for helping me. You are indeed an angel." And then Mary squeezed Lois's arm, motioned for her to bend down, and gave her a kiss on the cheek.

Lois wished Mary a safe flight and turned back down the walkway toward her gate. As she was walking, she thought that perhaps Mary should ask the customer-service agent if she could board early, as she would need assistance. She turned around and walked back to the gate. There was no line at the check-in counter. She looked for Mary in the waiting area, but she was nowhere to be found. She recognized the gentleman who had been standing in line in front of Mary when Lois left, and asked him if he had seen her after he checked in.

He looked at her, puzzled, and said, "I'm sorry, miss, but there was no one standing behind me in line. I was the last one."

Lois decided to look for Mary herself, so she checked the restroom and the waiting areas on both sides of the gate. But no Mary.

Then Lois smiled to herself, thinking that God works in mysterious ways. Mary was indeed with her on that beautiful day years ago, and she has felt her presence every day since.

Yes, Mother Mary *was* with Lois on that day, as she is with her every day, and with anyone who appeals to her for support. As an unlimited healer, Mother Mary can provide for everyone all at the same time. It doesn't matter *how* you call upon the Blessed Mother for help, but only that you do so, as the following story illustrates:

Jenn has had several visions of, and experiences with, Mother Mary; in fact, Mary was the first angelic ~~being~~ Jenn ever remembers seeing.

One evening in the early fall, Jenn was doing a meditation to help increase her intuition and psychic abilities. She was in a very relaxed state, which made it easy for her to just allow whatever came up to come up. She recalls seeing a rather tall spirit appear holding the hand of a small child. Jenn "knew" that this child was *her* some years prior.

This experience came to her at a time when she needed to do some healing with her inner child, and Mother Mary lovingly showed up to help her with this. Her energy was so pure and loving, and Jenn remembers the scene as if it were yesterday. Mary led her down the steps of a church, and out to meet with family members, who gathered around her.

In Mary's presence, Jenn felt so loved, and so confident in who she was. When she came out of that meditation, she felt peaceful and strong, and she knew that Mother Mary had performed a very powerful healing on her that evening. She thanked her gratefully for her love.

On another occasion, Jenn woke up one morning and rushed to work, but she felt off, as if something was nagging at her. She generally used her drive to work, which was over an hour on country roads, to do her morning prayers and affirmations. But something was different on this day. She was urged to pull her car over to the side of the road and do a very strong grounding exercise, which she did. Jenn started feeling very strong and connected, so she continued on her way.

The workday went smoothly, with no worries or concerns, so Jenn began to wonder why she had felt such a strong urge to get grounded. Then, once she got home, she received a call from a very close friend asking her not to contact him anymore. While this was hurtful, she also knew she had no choice but to accept his request and send him love and blessings.

Later that afternoon, she decided to take a nap, and she asked Mother Mary to be with her during this rest time. Jenn fell into a very peaceful sleep, and upon awakening, she felt herself wrapped in a cocoon of loving energy. At first, she lay there feeling the warmth of Mother Mary around her; then, as she slowly started to move, she could feel the cocoon being peeled away.

Jenn knew that a great healing had occurred during that rest period, so she was able to feel much more at peace with the message she'd received earlier in the day—as well as a heartfelt "knowing" that this was for her highest good. Jenn was so thankful for the time she spent in the arms of the Blessed Mother.

On yet another occasion, Mother Mary visited Jenn again during a meditation. This was a guided visualization, but for some reason, Jenn went off in a direction that did not follow the guide.

Jenn found herself in a wooded area, near a well of some type. She felt small, but as she looked down, she realized that she was still herself and was sitting in the lap of Mother Mary, who told her that she was going to wash away her sorrows. Mary proceeded to dip a sponge or cloth in the well and wash Jenn's heart.

She sat with Mother Mary for quite some time as she continued to wash and cleanse Jenn's heart. She could feel the purification and releasing taking place within her—an almost indescribable sensation. Before Mary left, she assured Jenn that many sorrows were gone, and that she was truly loved.

When Jenn came out of the meditation, she felt as though her heart had just been completely showered with love—as if so many troubling years of her life had been washed away. That evening she continued to send love and hugs to Mother Mary in gratitude for all that she had given her.

Although Jenn's spiritual practice is nontraditional, Mother Mary helped her as readily as she does everyone. She doesn't require us to pray in particular ways. The traditional prayers to Mother Mary are sacred tools to reach her; however, any heartfelt words that we're inspired to say are equally effective in eliciting her help. As the ultimate confidante and counselor, Mother Mary can be entrusted with our most private feelings. In fact, Mother Mary loves us unconditionally and without judgment, as a woman named **Scarlet** discovered:

Scarlet had lost just about everything in life that mattered to her, before she was helped by Mother Mary. First, she had to undergo a partial hysterectomy. Then, her husband got involved with drugs, and she lost her home and her marriage. And shortly after that, one of her children went to live with his father; meanwhile, she and her other child had to move in with her brother and sister-in-law. Scarlet felt that her life had become a total nightmare!

So she decided to start praying and meditating in her spare time. This inspired her sister-in-law to tell their church community that Scarlet was practicing witchcraft! In the Southern United States, where they lived, that kind of unfounded rumor can make you a pariah.

Anyway, one night Scarlet had a dream that changed things for her in an instant. She felt that she was a small child playing with her toys, and Mother Mary was on her bed, smiling and watching her.

Mary called out to her, and when she got up and went to her, Scarlet felt that they had become one energy. Scarlet wrapped her arms around her lovingly, and laid her head on the Blessed Mother's chest. She felt so safe and loved—something she had not felt in a very long time after losing everything in her life.

Mary told Scarlet that it was time for her to wake up and walk her true spiritual path. So, from that day on, that is exactly how Scarlet's life progressed. She started out taking baby steps, and although life wasn't easy, things did get so much better in so many ways.

Scarlet now feels that she is stepping 100 percent into her spirit self, and she is so glad she didn't do something rash like taking her own life, which is something she'd actually considered.

She will always be grateful to Mother Mary for putting her on the path of love and light.

As a nurturing mother figure, Mary boosts our self-acceptance and self-love. She did this for Scarlet by guiding her to align her life with her true spiritual beliefs and principles. If *you* need to increase your feelings of deservedness, ask Mother Mary for support. She will embrace you tenderly and help you see things in a new light, as she did for **Janna** and her marriage and family:

About three years ago, Janna went through a very stressful and emotional time in her life. Since she is a person who tends to keep personal problems inside, gathering so much pain into her heart was like a perpetual battle being waged within her.

Janna was considering divorcing her husband, although she remembers thinking that this notion was somewhat stupid, because everything seemed so wonderful on the surface. She blamed herself for being ungrateful for what she had: a partner and two wonderful children. She felt that she wouldn't be able to forgive herself for destroying her family, but she wasn't happy at all. Also, her daughter was just a baby, and Janna was terrified of being alone.

She'd had visions before, and usually they occurred at night, waking her up. Then Janna had two experiences on consecutive nights, which was unusual for her. The first night she woke up to a glowing, flaming light. She looked up at the closed bedroom door and there was an image reflected on its surface. It was a shadow of a big tree, and behind it was a huge sunset glowing all shades of orange. It disappeared fast, and she fell asleep again. To this day, she doesn't know the meaning of this vision, or whether it had something to do with what she was about to see the next night.

Janna woke up again in the middle of the night, feeling someone's presence in the room. She didn't see anyone as she looked up, so she went back to sleep. But then, the same feeling woke her up again, and she sensed a gentle light in the room, even though she had her eyes closed. As she opened them, Janna saw a lady's face. This wasn't just a vision or a picture—it was the clear presence of this lady. She had a gentle smile on her face, and a beautiful blue scarf around her head. The scarf was waving at the ends as if a light wind was blowing. It was a shade of blue Janna had never seen in her life, very difficult to describe.

This lady didn't say anything, nor did she have a message, but Janna felt a lot calmer and more peaceful after this experience. She just knew that everything was going to be all right, and that the problems in her family would be worked out.

It was a while after she'd met the mystery lady when she realized who it was. Janna saw a beautiful painting of Mother Mary with a blue scarf around her head, and knew that *she* had been the presence in her bedroom.

Now, every now and then when she needs help being more patient with her family, she calls upon Mother Mary to help her. After actually seeing the Blessed Mother, Janna has found it easier to recognize her presence. She always has a warm, motherlike, "hugging" energy.

The blue color of the scarf Janna saw is one of Mother Mary's signatures. As you'll read about later in this book, people who have Mary encounters and visions frequently report seeing a beautiful blue article of clothing or glowing blue light. Many describe the color as being "cornflower blue." As Janna said, it was a shade she'd never before seen.

Mary's healing energy is so strong that people can see the blue glow. They can also feel Mary's intense healing power, as a woman named **Ann** reported:

Ann had been helped on several occasions by Mother Mary. One example was when she was with a friend one day, chatting about a person whom she had experienced many challenging times with. Feelings of anger, sadness, and frustration bubbled up within her. Her friend suggested that Ann appeal to Mother Mary to help her find peace within herself, and to guide her whenever she felt those emotions surfacing.

So Ann sat quietly and asked for Mother Mary's healing energy. Suddenly, it was like a blanket of peace had come over her. It permeated every cell of her being. She had never felt such a profound sense of calm, and there was a stillness within her that was incredibly soothing. She didn't want that feeling to ever leave her, so she sat there as long as she could in order to soak it in.

Ann has asked Mother Mary for help on other occasions, and she has felt that same blanket of peace each time.

Mother Mary's calming and healing presence manifests whenever you call upon her. She is unlimited and unconditionally loving, so she's able to help everyone simultaneously.

Stella felt very blessed to have had a healing from Mother Mary, and she experienced a miraculous restoration of her faith immediately after. Previously, she had lost her faith, was totally disconnected from the Divine, and was in a dark place—feeling very angry, abandoned, and alone.

Stella was at a birthday gathering one day when she spoke to a friend, whom I'll call April, who practiced Pranic

Healing (an energy-healing method that I've personally enjoyed learning). April saw that Stella was depressed and offered to do a healing session on her right then and there. Stella accepted, but she was quite nervous about it, as she had never done something like that before.

They went into a bedroom, which felt kind of cold to Stella. But she followed April's instructions and sat with her eyes closed while her friend began the session. April asked her whom she felt connected to, in the spiritual realm, and without even thinking, Stella replied, "The Virgin Mary."

April smiled, and started to invoke Mother Mary for Stella's healing. Instantly, Stella saw the illuminated outline of Mother Mary in her mind's eye . . . and at the same time she saw it, her friend did, too! April said, "She's here with us now," and Stella knew that it was so.

As Stella started to feel calmer and less nervous, she realized that she was shivering from the cold of the bedroom, and her teeth were chattering. But in the next moment, she felt a warmth start to circulate in her chest. It was small at first, but began to enlarge and increase in temperature over the next minute or so. All of a sudden, she felt as if she were enveloped in heat similar to that of a sauna!

Stella thought, *Oh, I'm so hot!* and at that moment, her friend asked, "Can you feel the heat?"

Stella emphatically answered, "Yes!" She couldn't believe that she was so warm, when only moments before her teeth had been chattering from the cold! She felt as if she was being enfolded in a beautiful, loving, and compassionate hug from Mother Mary. It was heaven!

April then imparted a message from Mother Mary about Stella's son. Mary said that Stella must let go of her worry and guilt. Tears instantly began falling! (Stella's precious seven-year-old son had multiple severe life-threatening allergies and had to eat special foods. Stella's constant worry about him led her to lose faith and feel abandoned by God after many unanswered prayers for his healing.) She thought it was so beautiful that she and Mary, mother of Jesus, had connected as mothers with sons.

Stella walked out of that room a different person. She had regained her faith, and ever since, she has been taking many spiritual courses and has had many other illuminating experiences. Her child's condition has still not changed, and that remains a challenge, but Stella continues to pray for his overall health and protection.

We all know that faith is essential, and fortunately Mother Mary can restore our ability to trust, hope, and believe. Her presence is calming and healing, and gets us through life's difficult times, as **Michele Enli** can attest:

When Michele thinks about her childhood, all she remembers are snippets. Most of it is blacked out—and for good reason. She was abused as a child—sexually, physically, mentally, and emotionally.

One of the things she remembers is having a lot of tea parties and fun with her imaginary friend. She didn't know what had happened to her in her childhood for a long time—only that something *must* have transpired in order for most of her memories to be blacked out. In 2004, over 35 years after she had those tea parties, bits and pieces started to come out in dreams—a little at a time, and only enough for her to be able to handle at any given moment. From these tidbits, she was able to figure out what had happened to her.

Then she remembered her imaginary friend who had always been with her when she was a child. Oh, did they have fun! She could still see and feel those memories as if the events occurred yesterday. How they played, laughed, and laughed some more! When Michele had been with her friend, time had stood still.

She asked her mother if she remembered her having an imaginary friend growing up, and she said yes. Michele recalled that her friend's name was Mary. The more Michele thought about it, the more she *knew* it was Mary—Mother Mary! The Blessed Mother had been by her side through all those dark and challenging times as a child. And even now, Michele sees her in her visions. The Blessed Mother is guiding her and showering her with that special kind of motherly love that fills up her heart.

Michele hardly has the words to express how grateful she is to Mother Mary for all she has done for her, and continues to do! She knows that if it wasn't for Mother Mary, she wouldn't have made it through her childhood.

Michele constantly says, "God bless you, Mother Mary. I love you."

Mother Mary protects children vigilantly, even if she can't stop the freewill choices that abusive people make. Children such as Michele can feel or see Mary, and know that they're not alone.

Mother Mary's miracles of physical and emotional healing are available to everyone who calls upon her. As I've mentioned, it doesn't matter *how* you ask for her help, but only that you *do* ask for it. In the next chapter, we'll explore the special bond that Mother Mary has with all the children of the world.

CHAPTER FOUR

CHILDREN AND MOTHER MARY

Mother Mary is called "mother" because of her connection to children, especially baby Jesus. Most of us are familiar with the Christmas story in which the Archangel Gabriel announced to Mary that she would give birth to the Savior. This virgin birth is symbolic of the pure love within Mary's heart—a love she brings to children throughout the world, as the ideal mother.

Conception and Pregnancy

Mother Mary supports parents and children alike, beginning with conception and pregnancy.

For example, **Kimra Luna** has always felt a close connection to Mother Mary. She didn't know that it was okay to make contact with her until she started learning about communicating with the angels and ascended masters. Kimra began meditating with the intention of speaking to Mother Mary. She even used a candle with a Mother Mary image on it, to guide her meditation.

Kimra had questions about parenting, and she wanted to know if it was the right time for her to have another child. A few moments after she asked her questions, clear answers came to her. The pressure of the room changed, and Kimra began writing down everything she was feeling and hearing.

Mother Mary told her that all parents are meant to be as gentle as possible when it comes to child rearing, and should never manipulate their children with rewards and punishment. Mary told her that focusing on mutual cooperation works best in order to have a peaceful household. She also told Kimra that based on the way she was parenting, she would raise very spiritual, open-minded children who radiated love to all. Kimra was naturally quite pleased by all that Mother Mary had communicated to her.

Kimra then asked her if it was time for her to have a baby. Mother Mary told her she had been ready to be pregnant for months now, and to ask the angels for more information. So Kimra took out her angel oracle cards, and the first one she drew was "Children." She knew at that moment that she was already pregnant, and a test a few weeks later confirmed this.

Kimra now meditates and talks to Mother Mary whenever she has questions regarding parenting, relationships, or pregnancy. She feels very grateful for the connection she has with the Holy Mother, and for the wonderful guidance she is receiving.

In addition to conception, Mother Mary guides and supports women during their pregnancies and while giving birth.

In October 1996, **Margarita Guerrero** was pregnant with her fifth child, Maria Isabel. She went to the doctor on a Friday, about a week before the due date, but the baby was not in the right position to be born. Also, the baby was so big that the doctor said he was going to have to do a C-section. However, Margarita had already had a C-section with her second child, and she knew she didn't want another surgery.

She went home feeling sad, but then she started to pray. In fact, she prayed all weekend, asking Mary to help her, since she was the mother of Jesus and would understand the fear and anxiety she was going through. Margarita told the Blessed Mother that she trusted that she would be with her; and of course, as a good Catholic, she promised to name the baby Mary. Then she realized she was putting conditions on Mother Mary, so she told her that regardless of whether she received her help or not, the baby's name would be either Mary or Maria.

Margarita kept praying, and on Monday, she felt some pain, so she went to the doctor at 9 A.M. for further discussion about the C-section.

The doctor did an ultrasound and checked her over. He said that she was ready to deliver, and that she was already six or seven centimeters wide. He sent her directly to the hospital, and since Margarita only had minimal pain at this point, she thought she was going to be there all day.

She was admitted to the hospital at about 11 A.M. Two hours later, the nurse said she was going to call the doctor because Margarita was fully dilated. She was still having only minimal discomfort—no intense labor pains at all. The doctor checked her and said, "When you're ready, start pushing. The baby is ready to be born." She asked the doctor if he was sure she was in hard labor, and all he said was, "When you're ready, start pushing."

After two pushes, the baby was born. Margarita was in disbelief, as she had felt no pain. The baby was big—nine pounds, six ounces. Margarita hadn't told her husband about her promise to the Blessed Mother to name the baby Mary or Maria, so when she asked him what they should call their child and he said "Maria Isabel," at that moment she understood who had helped her with the delivery of her daughter. Mary had been with Margarita all day, looking after her so that she wouldn't have any pain and wouldn't need a C-section. This was an awesome confirmation of Mother Mary's presence, and every time Margarita looks at Maria Isabel, she remembers the miracle of her birth.

❦

Margarita knows that Mother Mary helped her welcome her beautiful daughter. When pregnancies have complications, the Queen of Angels is there to help, heal, and guide.

For example, during **Nelly Coneway**'s pregnancy, nothing could have prepared her for complications at birth. In the early morning of April 29, 1991, she felt her contractions start. Despite the cold, rainy day and the thick fog covering the city, she felt magic in the air. Something was telling her to expect a miracle.

In the hospital, even after hours of pain, there was no sign that her baby would arrive soon. As the doctors were examining Nelly, she read from their faces that something was very wrong, but the pain was unbearable, so she drifted away.

As if she were in a dream, she heard them saying: "We are losing both of them. The umbilical cord is tangled around the baby's neck. We need to do forceps, now!" The last thing Nelly remembers is praying to her angels and to Mother Mary to save her baby.

Later that day, Mother Mary, dressed in white and looking beautiful, woke Nelly up. She hovered above her, and rays of golden light illuminated the room, a contrast to the dark day outside. The love that was emanating from the Blessed Mother was overwhelming, and Nelly gratefully melted into her copper aura.

Mother Mary smiled at Nelly and said, "Congratulations. You gave birth to a beautiful boy. He is healthy and will bring many blessings to you and the world." Minutes later, the doctor came in to tell Nelly that she had a son. Without thinking, Nelly replied, "Yes, I know."

The doctor looked at her—stunned—but continued, "Your baby is in an incubator for observation because of complications with his breathing. He needs to stay here for two more weeks. What a lucky boy, though—he was born at 11:11 A.M."

Each day Nelly visited her son in the incubator and looked at his tiny body, sending him all her love and prayers for perfect health and strength. Somehow he reminded her of what had happened at her own birth. She had been born prematurely in the seventh month, and no-one thought she would make it, but she surprised everybody with her passion for life.

Thanks to Mother Mary and her angels, Nelly's son has grown up healthy and happy, and is now a smart, strong young man. Nelly will never forget that Mother Mary visited her in her hospital room and gave her the wonderful news about her son.

Like the world's most nurturing mother, Blessed Mary stands by the side of the woman giving birth, offering encouragement, guidance, and healing support.

Vicky, who lives in Greece, has always considered Mother Mary to be her protector and comforter in difficult situations. The week before Easter one year, she was pregnant with her son and went to the hospital on Wednesday to deliver him. She'd been waiting all night long, enduring one examination after another, and had received medication to help her deliver the baby. She went all night without sleep.

As morning came, and all of the other women in the ward had delivered their babies, Vicky became frustrated, so she prayed to Mother Mary, saying, "Today was the day your son was crossed [Holy Thursday in Greece is a very sacred day]. Please, Mother Mary, can you do something to help me give birth, or give me the strength to endure this?"

Five minutes later, Vicky's water broke, and she had a C-section. Everything went perfectly, and now her son is 15 and healthy. Vicky still prays to Mary when she needs comforting, as Our Lady feels like a mother to her.

❦

Mother Mary *is* a mother to Vicky. She's there for *all* of us, and especially for all the little children of the world. In fact, a woman named **Emma Kaiteie** knows for sure that Mother Mary has been with her during all of her pregnancies; however, she really came through for her in her second one.

Emma's gorgeous boy, Jack, was only eight months old when she got pregnant again with her beautiful girl, Penny. She was so excited, but at the same time so worried about how she would cope with a 17-month-old and a newborn—especially since her husband was studying and working as much as possible (sometimes 14-hour days). She realized she would have to cope a fair bit on her own. Emma was really quite stressed, and continually asked Mary and the angels for help.

One day early in her pregnancy, Emma found a beautiful cross on a chain in her jewelry box. In the center was an engraved image of Mother Mary's face outlined in blue, with pretty embossed markings down the length of the cross. Emma thought it must have belonged to her mother or one of her sisters, but no one had seen it before or knew to whom it belonged to.

To this day, Emma doesn't know where the cross came from. Her feeling is that Mary was giving her a physical sign that she was with her and supporting her, because when she wore the cross, she felt a sense of gentle strength within her. Emma wore it all through her pregnancy, and of course, things worked out beautifully.

Emma is now pregnant with her third child, and Mary has appeared repeatedly in her angel-card readings during times when she feels stressed and worried about the future. Emma feels safe, supported, and nurtured, knowing that Mary is with her.

༺༒༻

Mary *is* with Emma and her children, as well as with everyone in the world. To develop an even closer relationship with the Beloved Mother, just ask. She responds to every call for help.

Often, Mary answers our calls by giving us specific instructions that may not make sense at the time . . . but which are perfect answers nonetheless.

For instance, **Susie Garner** was nearly nine months pregnant and feeling increasingly uncomfortable about giving birth in the city she was living in. She was taking a nap one afternoon and woke up with the compelling feeling to go to a church in the little town called Adelaide Hills, near where she lived in Australia.

In this church, there had reportedly been sightings of Mother Mary, and Susie had visited it before with a friend and had felt Mother Mary's presence very strongly. So on this particular day, she got in the car, very pregnant, and drove to the church. No one was there, and as soon as Susie sat down, she felt the presence of the Blessed Mother. A river of tears flowed from Susie's eyes, and her heart ached as she connected with her gentle and oh-so-loving presence. She prayed to Mary to please give her guidance as to where she would be safe delivering her baby and it would feel right.

It was in the preceding hours that she'd begun to feel a certainty growing within her that it was best to stay with her sister and give birth in Melbourne. Later that night, she made the call to her sister, who flew over to accompany her on the plane ride to Melbourne. It was such a joyous release, as she felt the right answer come to her, thanks to the grace and nurturing love of Mother Mary.

Susie later reflected on why she was guided to her sister's home, and realized that the Blessed Mother was making sure she was secure and well looked after. You see, Susie was a single mother, and she ended up delivering her baby via C-section. So, if she'd stayed home and not gone to her sister's, she wouldn't have been able to look after herself or her children.

Mother Mary knows our probable future and foresees our needs, such as sending Susie to her sister's house. She also intervenes when a pregnancy or birth holds risk for the mother or baby, as she did for **Mary Ann Massey** and *her* mother:

Mary Ann was born into an Italian Catholic family, and her mother was 35 when she found out she was pregnant with her, which back in 1953 was cause for concern. She promised the Blessed Virgin that she'd name her child after her, in exchange for a healthy baby.

Mary Ann was born healthy, and was, of course, named for the Blessed Virgin. She always felt a connection to Mary, so during some very trying times when she was not only going through a divorce but was faced with the possibility of losing custody of her disabled son and his brothers, she often communicated with Mary. She always felt the Beloved

Mother's presence, which gave her reassurance that everything would be okay . . . and it was.

Ever-Present Childhood Help

After a child is born, Mother Mary continues to watch over the newborn and her family. As an example, **Nohelia L. deLaneuville**'s daughter Jessica was born in 1987, and she was a normal and beautiful baby. Nohelia wanted to breast-feed her daughter, but due to some medical complications, the doctor wanted the baby on formula.

Nohelia tried several different types of formula, but Jessica did not take to any of them well, as they would cause her to vomit and have diarrhea. She was losing fat and fluids, and Nohelia was very concerned.

One night Nohelia was crying while holding her baby daughter. She pressed Jessica to her heart and said a prayer to Mother Mary: "Dear Mother, you know how it feels to lose a child. I am putting my baby girl in your care. She is all I have. If she is going to heaven with you, please take good care of her!"

The next day, Nohelia was guided to try a new formula (the only one on the market she hadn't tried) and gave the bottle to her precious baby. Jessica took to it well, and although she did spit up a little, she drank it throughout the day and started improving immediately.

Jessica turned into a healthy, happy girl who is her mother's pride and joy, and Nohelia credits Mother Mary with making her baby well!

Nohelia and Jessica were helped out of a potentially dangerous situation with Mother Mary's guidance. Fortunately, Nohelia heard and followed the message to change formulas. If she hadn't, she might have mistakenly believed that her prayers went unanswered.

Nohelia's story perfectly illustrates how our prayers are often answered with intuitive thoughts and feelings to take action. When we do so, we work hand-in-hand with heaven to resolve the situation.

Mother Mary works with both the parent and directly with the child, to ensure that healing occurs. **Danielle Smutek**'s story is a remarkable illustration of how Mother Mary helps children:

Danielle was never one to push a religion or belief onto her child—she wanted that to be *his* decision. Although she had always been a very spiritual person she had never spoken to her son, Brock, about any of her beliefs before the following event occurred.

Brock had just turned four, and Danielle was going through a terrible breakup with his father. On this particular morning, she couldn't find her car keys. She was rummaging through everything, and she was swearing and yelling out of frustration.

Her son came up to her and said, "Mommy?"

"Yes, Brocky?" she asked.

He replied, "Say 'Heaven help me.'" Danielle didn't understand, and asked him to repeat what he'd said, so he did: "Say 'Heaven help me,' Mommy."

So she said, "Okay, heaven help me." Within minutes, she'd found the keys in the least expected place and definitely felt that she had been directed to them.

She asked her son where he had learned that phrase, and he replied simply, "From Mary, Mommy."

She asked, "Mary who?"

He answered, "Mary up in heaven with the angels, Mommy."

All of the hairs stood up on Danielle's arms, and she asked Brock to tell Mary that she said "Thank you." As Brock was walking away, she heard him say, "Mary, my mommy said 'Thank you.'"

Later that night, Danielle asked her son what Mary looked like, and he responded, "She's beautiful, Mommy. She looks like a princess and wears all blue."

She also asked him how he knew her, and he replied, "From before I was born, Mommy."

Danielle's eyes filled up with tears, and she thanked little Brock for choosing her to be his mommy.

This experience stayed on her mind for days, and she couldn't let it go, so one afternoon she decided to test her son's knowledge. She pulled up a picture of Mother Mary on the Internet while her son was nearby. Danielle asked him to look at the computer screen and asked, "Brocky, can you tell me who this is?"

His eyes lit up, and with a huge smile, he unhesitatingly said, "That's Mary, Mommy. I know her." Then she pulled up a picture of Jesus and asked him who *that* was, and he replied, "That's the King of Heaven, Mommy."

There is no way her son could have known any of this, which makes it so astounding and so miraculous!

Children are naturally spiritually gifted, so they can see Jesus, Mother Mary, and angels. When parents like Danielle praise their children for their spiritual gifts, they are encouraged to stay connected to heaven.

Blessed Mother Memories from Childhood

Childhood fears are normal, but fortunately Mother Mary is readily available to soothe and comfort little ones. As people grow up, they always remember the times when Mother Mary came to their aid during childhood. For instance, when **Jamain Brigitha** was four years old, she had a vivid dream of the Virgin Mary on the yellow veranda of her home. It was during a time when her mother and father were getting divorced, and there was a lot of turmoil around her. The light and glowing presence of the Blessed Mother felt protective, and she has never forgotten this image, and the comforting safety that Mother Mary brought her.

Because of her dream, Jamain grew up knowing that Mother Mary was watching over her. This gave her comfort and helped her enjoy a feeling of safety and happiness.

Children's faith is so pure and complete. They really believe, and their faith is often rewarded with instant and miraculous healings, as **Connie McCowan** remembers from her childhood:

As a three-year-old, Connie suffered from a rare form of infantile eczema, a chronic disorder that involved a painful hypersensitivity of the skin on both arms.

Twice daily she would have her arms carefully scrubbed, then medicated, prior to having the exposed raw areas of skin wrapped in white medical strips.

One Friday evening while her father was getting her ready for bed, Connie cried out loudly, "Daddy, this hurts so much! How can I make it go away?"

He told her to pray to Our Blessed Holy Mother by asking her to heal her arms, then pray three Hail Marys. Connie asked her father to help her, so they kneeled together and asked Mother Mary to heal her by removing the painful rash from her arms, and then they prayed three Hail Marys.

After the prayers, Connie's father tucked her into bed, where she anxiously waited for her healing. The following morning, she eagerly asked her mother to remove her bandages so she could see her arms. They went to the bathroom, and Connie's mother removed the bandages, then gasped. She began to tremble, and started screaming and crying. Her father and siblings ran into the bathroom to see what all the commotion was about, and Connie's mother started jumping up and down, exclaiming, "Her arms are clear—they're healed!" over and over.

Connie's father started weeping, then said, "Coneka [the nickname he had given her at birth], your prayers have been answered."

She replied with confidence, "I know, because I prayed." From that moment on, Connie considered herself a Mama's girl—a "Holy Mama's girl."

I imagine how Connie and her parents must have felt to experience this miraculous healing. It must have also given them comfort during life's trying moments, since they all realized that miracles really *do* occur. **Jolanta Robertson** and her sister also received miracle healings due to Mother Mary's Divine intervention:

Jolanta and her sister were both very young when they contracted either scarlet fever or something equally serious. They lived in Sopot, Gdańsk, Poland (a block away from the Baltic Sea). Jolanta was a year and a half older than her sister, Leila, and they were both very sick. In fact, it was believed that they wouldn't survive.

Their mama went crazy, crying and tearing out her hair when this was unfolding. She fell on her knees and prayed and cried to Mary to spare her daughters' lives. That night, she had a dream that Mother Mary was standing above their cribs with her hands outstretched to let her know that she was taking care of her children.

Their mama woke up and went running to the girls' cribs to find that their fevers had broken, and both Jolanta and Leila were healthy and sleeping peacefully.

It was a miracle that she will never forget—and neither will her daughters.

❧

Mother Mary's healing miracles extend to emotional wellness, as she reassures us and calms away childhood fears:

Monique is a highly sensitive person who was a fearful child. Even when there was nothing going on, she had a nervousness inside of her, but she found it difficult to talk about these feelings. Her mother was loving but also highly sensitive, so Monique didn't want to upset her by letting her know that she wasn't feeling well inside.

Then one time when her family was on a vacation in the woods, Monique had a restless night. In the early-morning hours, she felt nerves swirling through her body. Suddenly, on the left side of her bed, Mother Mary appeared. Monique recognized her immediately. She wore a red, white, and blue robe, and her hair was dark brown. Her eyes were pools of gentleness. Monique was surprised at the time that she wasn't taller, but she later understood that Mary didn't want to scare Monique by appearing larger.

Mary raised the two fingers of her right hand and gave Monique a blessing. She said, "I will be your mother in need." The Holy Mother explained that she would be there for Monique and her family, especially when they wouldn't be able to express themselves. She would be the silent Mother Who Speaks.

It was exactly what Monique needed to hear, because she often had a hard time expressing herself, and she knew that it was the same for her father, mother, and brother. To this day, her family members find great comfort in Mother Mary—especially her mentally disabled brother, who is fragile and has a hard time dealing with his emotions. He feels supported by his earthly and heavenly mother, because he knows that he is understood.

As Monique discovered, Mother Mary helps with every healing need. Her outpouring of compassion makes the Blessed Mother's gifts that much more potent, because they're given to us with unconditional love.

The comfort that Mother Mary bestows upon us is so pure and powerful that it melts away all fears. Even her presence fills the air with warmth, as **Samantha Anear** recalls from her childhood:

When she was in lower primary school (she was either five or six years old), Samantha had two cousins who were training hands-on to become nurses. They were always so happy and full of fun, but on this particular day, there were no smiles to be seen.

It was bedtime, and at this point in her life, Samantha was sharing a bedroom with her brother, Peter. They were whispering quietly to each other, as they knew something was going on between their parents and their cousins, who had shut all the doors so that the kids wouldn't be able to hear what they were discussing.

Apparently, on that day, her cousins had experienced the death of a patient—the first time that had occurred. Samantha never found out exactly what had happened, but she did know that there were lots of tears and drinking, and it went on for quite a while!

Samantha was still whispering to Peter and only realized that he was asleep after the long pause in their conversation. Her stomach was all knotted up, and she wasn't sure how to feel, as she had not really experienced death personally and was picking up on all the vibes that were in the house, making it impossible for her to sleep. She lay listening for what seemed like an eternity and then heard the scraping of chairs on the floor, meaning that her cousins were leaving.

Samantha snuck through all the closed doors and out the front door (left ajar by her parents) and was intending to go through the garden gate and into the courtyard to say good-bye to her cousins and make sure they were going to be okay. Before she got to the gate, she felt a warmth surround her. She knew that it was very late at night, and it was cold and all she was wearing was a cotton nightie, but she felt so cozy—like she was being enveloped in a big, warm cuddle!

She saw a beautiful radiant blue gown on her right-hand side, and just knew that it was Mother Mary. She had the most amazing smile, which brought Samantha comfort, and her anxiety dissipated. Samantha never heard the Blessed Mother's words with her ears—it was if she *felt* them with her heart: "Fear not, my child, as death is only a small step in life, and is a lesson that will be learned by all."

Samantha had no questions, as she felt that this was true, and was all that needed to be said. "Thank you, Mother Mary," she whispered. She knew that her cousins were going to get over this, and that there was nothing to fear.

Samantha found it hard to go back into the house and return to bed, but she felt a warm hand on the middle of her upper back, guiding her back inside.

She feels honored that Mother Mary communicated with her in this way, and cherishes this memory, which will reside deep in her heart for as long as she lives.

Sadly, for some children, Mother Mary is the only trustworthy adult figure they can call upon. When **Sharon Duquette** was a little girl, she would pray to the Blessed Mother all the time. She can't really remember exactly how old she was when she began doing so or why she felt so connected to her, but what she does know is that she felt safe, loved, and protected whenever she thought of Mary.

There were many problems in Sharon's home when she was growing up—lots of fighting and screaming. And since she was a really sensitive child, this frightened her more than she ever admitted or realized. When she got older, she learned how to conceal this side of herself well; but when she was young, she was very afraid of all the yelling, and she would often run and hide in her bedroom closet to get away the noise.

At some point, she began praying to the Blessed Mother. This isn't something she ever shared with anyone, because as a child, she thought she was doing something wrong by praying only to Mother Mary, thinking that God would be mad at her and punish her for not praying "the right way." At times she would ask God for forgiveness for praying "wrong," and she would explain that it was because she felt so close to Mary, who made her feel so loved and safe.

Many years ago, Sharon went through a series of very trying and difficult times. Her brother died, which led her to become sick, both mentally and physically. Sharon felt like her world was crumbling all around her, so she took a leave of absence from her job and began an inner search for healing. She began praying to the Blessed Mother again for guidance. Looking back now, she sees how everything around her had to crumble to get her back to her inner faith.

As Sharon's story poignantly illustrates, Mother Mary gives us comfort and support during life's trials. She also helps us find spiritual meaning amid tragedies. How wonderful that parents teach their children to pray, and give them these important tools for living.

That's exactly what **Edward Yagger**'s mother did, in fact. When Edward was a child, his mother would always tell him, "Ed, pray to Mother Mary, and she will answer your prayers." Being young, with the world in front of him, he didn't pay attention. Over the years, he and his mother grew apart, but each time she would call him on the phone, the conversation would always end with her saying: "Ed, don't forget to pray to Mother Mary."

When his mother passed away, it was at a time when they were having a falling-out and not talking to each other. Edward was stunned, realizing that he would never have the chance to make amends or tell his mother how much he loved her. This left him in a very sad and disoriented state of mind.

One day while walking down the street, Edward came across a picture of Mother Mary in a window and heard his mother's voice say: "Pray to Mother Mary." So that night he went home and did just that.

After several months of praying, one night he was awakened by someone tapping his toe (only his mother had done that when he was young). Edward opened his eyes, wondering who had touched him, as he didn't have any pets or roommates. Thinking he was dreaming, he went back to sleep, only to have his toe tapped again. He sat up suddenly, sure of what he had just felt!

On the wall in front of his bed, there was a mist or fog forming. He immediately thought it was smoke from a fire, but then he saw an image of Mother Mary on his wall, and she was smiling down at him. Edward rubbed his eyes in disbelief and then saw his mother quietly standing next to Mary, also smiling! Thinking he was losing his mind, he at last heard a female voice say three times: "Your mother is with me, and everything will be fine."

After the vision disappeared, he lay back down, stunned, but feeling warm, peaceful, and calm. From that day forward, Edward has prayed to Mother Mary, and has expressed his gratitude to her for the incredible gift of love and closure she gave him.

What a compassionate gift Mother Mary bestowed upon Edward, relieving him of suffering from grief and guilt over his relationship with his mother!

Children aren't emotionally equipped to deal with death and loss, so they need the additional support that Mother Mary provides, as **Amanda Dowell**'s story illustrates:

Mother Mary came to Amanda at a time when she was very sad. She was seven years old, and her grandmother had just passed away.

Amanda's grandmother knew from the time her granddaughter was born that she was very sensitive, and that her spiritual gifts should be encouraged to flourish. Grandma felt that Amanda's connection to God was so special that she knew things others could not. This gift could have been considered negative, but Grandma took a different approach, believing that her granddaughter was a child of the Divine light of the Creator.

Anyway, on the day Grandma died, Amanda sensed the presence of a woman who looked just like a mother. The woman comforted Amanda, telling her that everything was going to be all right. Later that day, Amanda was told by her own mother that Grandmother Dorothy was gone.

But Amanda didn't want to believe it. She was so mad at God that her grandma had been taken from her. When Amanda was alone in her room, the motherly woman she had seen earlier came in and said to her, "Dear child, I am Mother Mary, and I bring you what you have asked for." In walked Grandmother Dorothy to tell her that she hadn't gone anywhere—she had just been on a trip, and Amanda was the only one who could see her!

Amanda realized that Grandma was now guiding her, and Mother Mary was along to comfort her. Grandma said, "Young child, you are a child of light, and you are connected to the Divine." Ever since then, Amanda's grandma and Mother Mary have been by her side.

Losing a loved one can turn anyone's world upside down, especially that of a child who doesn't understand life and death. That's why Mother Mary steps in to help grieving children, as she did for **Emmy** when she was eight years old:

Emmy was a very religious child who attended a Catholic primary school in the country, and her teachers would always comment on how spiritual she was and just how seriously she took her connection with Mother Mary, Jesus, and all the saints.

When other kids in her classroom would read comic books, Emmy would be flipping through heavy, dusty tomes about the saints. She was intellectually, emotionally, and spiritually absorbed with and inspired by how the saints lived and what their message was for the world. The spiritual journey they traveled completely intrigued her as a child, and still does.

Emmy's teachers were convinced that she would grow up to be a nun. (She did in later years receive a spiritual calling, but it was a little different than expected—she became a spiritual healer.)

So, as a young child, Emmy talked endlessly to her angels and would pray all the time—in the morning, all day at school, when she got home, and especially at night before she fell asleep. She would always sense her guardian angels at the end of her bed, watching and protecting her through the night as she slept.

But Emmy's faith in the world was shaken when her mother delivered a stillborn baby. Emmy buried herself in the religious aspects of school and prayed incessantly. She knew that the infant was safe in heaven (having had visions of people in spirit since she was five years old), and she believed in the existence of angels, because she'd seen them with her own eyes, but she felt like she needed more of a sign to let her know that the departed baby was in safe hands.

Her grandmother taught her a lot about Jesus and Mary and gave her a book about the Holy Mother. Emmy fell in love with Mary and the stories about her, and she vowed as an eight-year-old that she wanted to be just like her.

Emmy prayed every night, and really poured her whole heart and soul into the prayers she was sending to Mary. Her grandmother told her about her visitation from Saint Thérèse at the funeral of her grandfather, where roses and rose petals were left everywhere—in her home, at the cemetery, and in places she didn't expect to discover them. She would find a rose and know that it was a sacred sign from Saint Thérèse, the "Little Flower." Her grandmother had had many visitations from the saints—to help her conceive and raise her children and to help her through her grief; and she told Emmy that if she prayed hard enough with her whole heart, she too would be blessed with miracles in her life.

Mother Mary visited Emmy on a Friday night, and she will never forget it. She had spent the previous three nights praying to Mary for three hours at a time, really pouring her young heart out. She truly believed with all her heart that she was speaking with a gentle mother who loved her so much.

On the night of the visitation, Emmy was tucked in her bed in the room she shared with her sister, and once again she was praying with her whole heart. The hallway light streamed through the crack in the door, and she felt more alone than usual.

Emmy had been praying for about 20 minutes, her tears still warm and wet on her cheeks, when all of a sudden she noticed the room get darker yet more vivid, with a sharpened focus. Her eyes were wide open, and all of sudden out of nowhere, she saw a bubble of light, white in the center with edges of yellow all around it.

Inside the bubble of light was Mother Mary. She was dressed in a blue gown, and she had the most kindly, sincere face. She spoke to Emmy for a few minutes in the softest voice. She kept calling her "my child." She then assured her that everything was okay with her grandfather and with the baby, and that she had heard her prayers and Emmy wasn't to be afraid.

Emmy felt so close to that warm bubble of light, as if she could just reach out and touch it. It radiated pure love, compassion, and gentle kindness. Mother Mary stayed for a few minutes, and then the bubble of light slowly dimmed and faded into the darkness of the room.

Emmy lay there, stunned by what she had seen, knowing that she had just had a very sacred and spiritual experience. She felt blessed that she had connected with Mother Mary, and was comforted, knowing that her relatives were safe in heaven, in the gentle hands of a loving mother.

Emmy ran into her mom's room and woke her up, telling her about her heavenly experience. They held each other and cried. It was a very special night that Emmy will never forget as long as she lives.

Instead of "solving" a problem, Mother Mary helps us cope with life's challenges. With her strong and gentle presence, the Blessed Mother allows us to feel safe. She gives us the courage to persevere, like only a loving parent can do.

In the next chapter, we'll explore how Mary helps mothers enjoy and fulfill their sacred parenting roles.

CHAPTER FIVE

MARY MOTHERHOOD

As the mother of Jesus, Mary is revered as *the* mother. Her ideal maternal qualities of loving-kindness, such as being nurturing, caring, and calm, are simultaneously accessible to *all* mothers.

For example, many women worry whether they're "good enough" mothers. They carry guilt that they're not doing all they can for their children, or are anxious that they're making parenting mistakes. Fortunately, Mother Mary can reassure these mothers, as she did with **Jeanean Mitchell:**

Jeanean has two sons who are 11 and 13, but when they were babies, she wondered what kind of mother she was—that is, was she being a good role model, was she doing them justice, did she love them the "right way"? Certainly, these are concerns that a lot of mothers have.

One night Jeanean had a dream that wasn't like any other she'd ever had. This one seemed to go on for the entire time she was asleep. She remembered having a conversation with Mother Mary, and woke up still talking to her. She doesn't really remember all of it, but she recalls the *feeling* of it—as if she were being told that she was on the right course with her sons and needed to be strong, firm, yet loving with the two boys.

It was the most calming and soothing experience she'd ever had in a dream, and there were no strange elements that didn't make sense. It was as if Jeanean and Mary had sat down and had a conversation all night long.

Now, when her boys throw her for a loop, she goes back to that feeling, and is very grateful for it.

Mother Mary has the calming and soothing effect that Jeanean described, whether she comes to you while praying, meditating, or dreaming. She works side by side with human mothers to calm and heal their children when they're frightened or ill, as **Lori-Elizabeth N. Coleman** recalls from her childhood:

When Lori-Elizabeth was five years old, she had a high fever, having caught the latest illness that had swept through her kindergarten class. That night, the light in the hallway was on, and Lori-Elizabeth's mother had moved her bed so she could see her from the hall when she woke up. Lori-Elizabeth's bedroom door was open, and she was wide-awake.

She turned her head to look into the hallway, and in front of her door was a silhouette of a woman. Her robe was swirling with the most beautiful colors Lori-Elizabeth had ever seen. The woman's palms were turned outward at her side, and when she moved her head, she was radiating! She looked at Lori-Elizabeth for a moment and then smiled. Lori-Elizabeth's fever broke, and she was instantly well. Seconds later, the beautiful woman disappeared.

Lori-Elizabeth told the story to her mom, who smiled at her daughter but offered no explanation. When Lori-Elizabeth asked her mom about it years later, she said she thought it was Mother Mary who had visited her that night, and to this day, Lori-Elizabeth feels a special connection to her. She knows how blessed she is to have Mother Mary as one of her many guardians.

❧

Mother Mary is able to be with *all* children and mothers who need her help. She is the ultimate multitasker. As you'll read in the following story, single mother **Karen Clothier** wisely asked Mother Mary to co-parent with her:

A couple years ago, Karen asked God, Mother Mary, and the angels to bring her and her two sons together to a place in Maine that was always very special to them, as she'd taken them there every year to play at the beach.

After her sons grew older, Karen needed help, because they were starting to drive and be independent, and as a single mother, she still worried about them. So, she began to ask Mother Mary to watch over her boys, especially her oldest, Zack.

Well, the angels did get the three of them to Maine, and one beautiful evening on that special beach where they had spent some amazing summer vacations, Karen was silently thanking God, Mother Mary, and the angels for bringing them together. As she turned to look at Zack, she saw the most amazingly beautiful blanket of blue surrounding his head, from one side of his neck, up around his face, and down to the other side of his neck.

Karen strongly felt the presence of Mother Mary, and believes that this was her way of letting her know that she was watching over her son. Karen felt a sense of overwhelming peace that she had never experienced before, and she considers it a wondrous miracle.

Mother Figure for All

Some children don't have an appropriate maternal influence in their lives. Perhaps their mother is incapacitated by illness or addiction, or has moved or passed away. The grieving child can call upon Mother Mary to fulfill the need for a mother figure.

Mother Mary has been in **Aurelia**'s life from the start, guiding her since she was about two years old. Her mother had left her and her brother in Mexico with her aunt while she came to the U.S. to seek a better life for them. Her mother had always told her she looked like *la Virgen María,* and had given her a framed picture of Mary to help her while she was away.

For two long years, Mother Mary became Aurelia's "mother." She spoke to the Blessed Mother daily, cried and laughed as she shared her day with her, slept with that picture, and felt that anything she needed was there for the asking.

Aurelia fully believed that Mother Mary helped her make it through that first storm in her life. She prayed that her mother would come get her and her brother, and two years later, the family was finally reunited and moved to the States.

These days, there is a connection with Mother Mary that fills Aurelia with an indescribable sense of love and peace. She see Mary's image everywhere—in the clouds, on tiles, on ceilings—and she sees roses even when they're not in season and where they wouldn't be expected to appear. Aurelia knows they are a sign that Mother Mary will be with her always, and that no matter how difficult life gets, the Blessed Mother will be her beacon of light!

If your mother isn't physically available to you, you can ask Mother Mary for maternal nurturing, as **Joëlle Guillemette** discovered:

Joëlle and her sister moved in with their father when she was eight years old. She relied a lot on her big sister because their mother wasn't around. When Joëlle was 13, her sister moved away, and she ended up living alone with her father. He worked the night shift, so she was by herself a lot. Although her dad was very loving, compassionate, and funny, it just wasn't the same as having a woman around. She missed the motherly hugs and kisses, especially when she was sick or sad.

One night Joëlle was talking to God and Mother Mary, and she asked the Blessed Mother if *she* could be her mom, since her own wasn't around much. From then on, Joëlle would turn to the Blessed Mother often. Then, when she had her own daughters, she also turned to Our Lady for motherly help. There came a day when she made the decision for her oldest daughter to go live with her friends for a year to help her at school, because the schools in their city were letting her fall desperately behind in her education. The day that Joëlle's daughter left, she cried the whole night while talking to God, Mother Mary, and Jesus.

But then she suddenly felt so loved, and in her mind's eye she saw Mother Mary on one side of her and Jesus on the other, and they held her all night. She remembers the comforting hug so well.

Joëlle purchased some pink silk roses that she keeps on a shelf at her bedside, and she calls on Mother Mary often, knowing that she's always listening.

The faith that Joëlle feels, knowing that Mother Mary is with her, gave her a foundation throughout her childhood and into adulthood. No matter what your relationship with your mother is like, the Blessed Mother can provide for you. I just love the following story in which Mother Mary provided love to a teenage girl:

Talua Manning's experience with Mother Mary occurred when she was 16, and it really moved her. Talua's mom used to come into her room at bedtime and kiss her good night. After going to sleep one evening, Talua remembers waking ever so slightly to the feeling of being kissed on her forehead, and watching a beautiful lady slowly fade toward the back of her room and disappear into the corner.

The next morning, Talua woke up and asked her mother if she had kissed her good night. Her mom told her, "No, sorry, I didn't."

Talua then explained to her mom what she had seen and felt, and they both smiled. Talua didn't realize until a few years later that the lovely lady was Mother Mary. To this day, that image remains a precious memory in her head and heart.

Mary Heals Motherly Grief

Parenting comes with emotional highs and lows, but nothing can compare to the pain of losing a child. Whether a son or daughter passes during pregnancy or in childhood, the sorrow is intense and lasting. Fortunately, Mother Mary comforts grieving parents so that they can go on with their lives, and feel some semblance of peace.

For example, **Mary Alice Santoro** had always been a late bloomer. She got married at age 35, not because she was fussy, but because she was waiting for the right man to come into her life—her soul mate—and she finally found him. When she became pregnant five months after the wedding, she and her husband were thrilled. They told everyone it was a gift from God.

However, their joy turned to sorrow when Mary Alice miscarried about six weeks later. Grief-stricken, she asked

God why He had given her a baby and then taken it away. But she received no answers.

The doctors found nothing wrong with her, saying, "It was just one of those things." *One of those things?* Mary Alice simply couldn't accept that explanation. If there was no *physical* reason, then there had to be a metaphysical or spiritual one. She continued to grieve—often crying in the bathroom so as not to upset her husband. She also continued to ask God why this had happened.

Then one night in a dream, she got her answer. She saw Mother Mary, and she was holding an infant wrapped in a blanket. She was some distance away, but Mary Alice knew that the baby the Blessed Mother was holding was hers. Mother Mary was wearing a long blue dress and a white veil. Her hair was brown and shoulder length.

So softly and sweetly, Mother Mary said to her, "My child, do not grieve so. This baby is a child of God, as are you. She is well cared for and loved. She is praying for you and will always be with you. All is well."

This happened 25 years ago, and Mary Alice has never forgotten how beautiful Mother Mary was and how much love radiated from her. Mary Alice moved on with her life, secure in the belief that she has her own angel in heaven praying for her . . . and that we all have a Loving Mother watching over us who wants us to be happy.

How compassionate of Mother Mary to give Mary Alice a vision of her baby cradled in heaven, knowing that this sight would comfort a grieving mother. Mother Mary performed a similar miracle for **Sandra McLean**, even before she lost her baby:

In 2006 Sandra became pregnant somewhat unexpectedly. One night in the early weeks of her pregnancy, the Blessed Mother came to her in a dream. Sandra instantly knew her, as Mary was sitting on a large throne among white clouds, holding a baby wrapped in a pink blanket.

Mother Mary smiled so warmly, and spoke to Sandra without words, saying that she would keep this baby close to her and would care for her, as it was not her time to come to Earth. When Sandra woke up, she realized that she had starting bleeding. She miscarried a few days later.

It was very sad, and Sandra had two more miscarriages, but she knew within the depths of her soul that the Divine Mother was watching over her—and all of us. Sandra is certain that Mary guides us and puts light on our path, according to our Divine plan.

Sandra often prays to the Blessed Mother, and always finds such peace and love when thinking about her.

As soon as a mother conceives, she bonds with her baby, and losing a child is painful no matter when it happens. Thank heaven that Mother Mary supports mothers through their grief.

On Australia Day (January 26), 2007, **Carly Marie Dudley** gave birth to her stillborn son, Christian. His life had ended before it had a chance to begin. As Carly held his lifeless little body against her chest, she prayed to Mother Mary. She had felt drawn to pray to her ever since she had become a mother for the first time in 2006. She was experiencing the ultimate grief, and she knew that the Blessed Mother would understand the pain of losing a child.

Carly lay in her hospital bed with her eyes closed and asked Mary and the angels to come and take her beautiful son to heaven. When she opened her eyes, she saw the brightest light flash out of the room. It was as if a light had been turned on, and then all of a sudden at the moment she opened her eyes, someone had switched it off. Carly felt sure that Mother Mary had come to take her baby to heaven, and she felt a sense of peace at that moment that she cannot describe adequately in words.

Knowing that her son was with Mother Mary allowed Carly to grow into the mother and woman she is today. She rose above her grief and is now helping thousands of families from all over the world be at peace after losing children, by creating International Bereaved Mothers Day on the first Sunday of every May.

How beautiful that Carly transformed her pain into a platform for helping other grieving mothers. Mother Mary may not be able to prevent all deaths from occurring, but she can help heal the suffering occasioned by a child's passing.

Connie Misiolek's mother has always been a faithful woman, and she still prays the Rosary at least three times a day, even at the age of 92.

Back in May of 1956, before Connie was born, her mom woke up one morning to the sound of leaves blowing and a rustling on the other side of the door to her room. The door slowly opened, and in walked the Blessed Mother. Her mom sat up, amazed. She said that Mother Mary, who looked sad, had her hands folded in prayer and was holding a string of rosary beads. Behind her, Connie's mom said she saw herself in a particular dress, her husband in a particular suit, and her daughter wearing her Communion gown, but she did not see her six-year-old son. This concerned her, so she went to discuss this dream/vision with her good friend who lived across the street (who eventually became Connie's god-mother). This friend told her not to worry, because school would be out soon, and she could keep a better eye on her little boy.

Two months later, on July 12, 1956, Connie's mom went to her friend's house for just a few minutes, telling her son to stay home and that she would be right back. Unfortunately, the little boy didn't listen. He went outside, crossed the street, and was struck and killed by a car. Connie's sister witnessed this and was the one to tell their mom that "someone ran over Lenu" (a Polish nickname for Leonard). At his funeral Connie's mom wore that particular dress, her father wore that particular suit, and her sister wore the Communion gown seen in the vision.

In the card Lenu had given Connie's mother for Mother's Day that year, he had signed it: "Love, Lenu. I will see you in heaven." Not a typical thing for a six-year-old to say.

Connie's mom is convinced to this day that Mother Mary was preparing her for her beloved son's death, and that he *will* be with her in heaven.

❧

Knowing that a child is watched over by Mother Mary is comforting for grieving parents, who might otherwise worry about the child's afterlife fate. Mother Mary also brings reassurance to women who'd like to be mothers but cannot conceive.

Stacy Corley was raised Catholic and always had a close relationship with Mother Mary. Stacy is unable to have children. Recently she was having a sad moment with her eyes closed, and she saw Mary standing behind her with her hand on her left shoulder. She was so loving and so supportive, and she has stepped in many times to help Stacy with her personal healing.

Stacy has accepted the fact that Mother Mary is always with her and has become one of her guides. Sometimes the Holy Mother appears to her with a soft giggle . . . as well as a smile, a wink, and a nod.

Stacy is filled with gratitude for the close connection she has with Mary. She has helped her deal with not having children by showing her that one can be a mother to *all*. She has a mothering relationship with her two dogs and many people, which helps her nurturing needs feel satisfied.

The Blessed Mother is beloved by all whose lives she touches with her gentle, caring spirit. With her infinite ability to help countless people at once, Mother Mary provides comfort, healing, and—as you'll read in the next chapter—protection. After all, to Mother Mary, we are her children. She can foresee potentially dangerous situations, and she's able to give lifesaving warnings.

CHAPTER SIX

PROTECTED BY MOTHER MARY

The watchful eye of the Blessed Mother shields us from harm through miraculous Divine intervention. In this chapter, you'll read more about Mother Mary's protective, and even lifesaving, presence. In some cases, she issues warnings and guidance that—when followed—result in a return to safety. In other instances, Mother Mary appears as a vision or through her classic signs: blue lights and the fragrance of roses. Often, logic is defied as someone walks away from accidents unscathed or heals miraculously. All of these protection experiences are born of the great love Mother Mary shares with everyone.

For example, a woman named **Rebecca** received reassurance from Mother Mary, which gave her courage and faith during an automobile accident:

On June 25, 2001, Rebecca was driving home from work on a highway in Norfolk, Virginia. It was about 7 in the evening, and the sun was at such an angle that it was difficult to see. An accident occurred right in front of her, and she knew she didn't have enough room to brake, as she was traveling at 55 miles per hour.

Somehow she managed to stop her car within a foot of the vehicle in front of her, and then an overwhelming sense of peace came over her. This peace was accompanied by the smell of roses, and she heard a voice say, "I am Mary. Everything will be fine."

Almost as soon as Rebecca heard those words, she was rear-ended and pushed into the accident in front of her. She didn't feel anything, but she could hear the crunch of metal as her car's frame was bent and twisted.

She again heard the words "Everything will be fine," and knew that the voice was right. Once the car door was pried open by two very strong police officers, Rebecca was able to exit what could only be described as a mangled piece of metal. However, she did not have a scratch on her. Her boss, who had traveled past the scene, commented to her the next morning: "I was certain you must be dead, as no one could have walked away from that accident."

Rebecca is certain, too . . . that it was Mother Mary who spoke those comforting words and assured her she'd be okay. And she was.

Protective Warnings

Mother Mary does speak reassurance to us, as well as prophetic warnings that keep us safe and protected. For example, registered nurse **Karen Bishop** narrowly avoided a tragedy because she listened to the Blessed Mother's cautionary advice:

At a very young age, Karen felt a strong connection to the Holy Mother. Often she'd think of visiting Lourdes to be closer to Mary—and she finally realized that dream in 2004.

Karen's early home life was very chaotic, so she would often pray to Our Lady and pour her heart out. When she was 12 years old, she had gone to sleep on a bitterly cold winter night in upstate New York. Her grandmother had bought her an electric blanket, and she made sure it was on a medium setting.

After a while in the dream state, she "saw" the Holy Mother, who was speaking to her. Mary was off in the distance and kept repeating, "Karen, wake up, wake up!" Karen awoke from a deep sleep feeling a sharp pain on her thigh, and when she opened her eyes, the room was full of smoke—the electric blanket had caught fire! Within a few moments, her parents rushed into her room; they were coughing and gasping from the smoke, and somehow her dad put the fire out.

Karen told her mom and dad what had happened, but she didn't think they believed her. However, *she* knew it was real, and to this day, she hasn't forgotten how Our Lady watched over her, her parents, and the little apartment they lived in so none of them would be harmed.

Karen has no doubt that the Blessed Mother's presence is real . . . and a source of love and protection for all.

I have no doubt, either. After all, Mother Mary will do anything to keep us all safe, healthy, and happy, without violating our freewill decisions. It makes sense that she issues loud and clear warnings that we can hear over the din of fearful emotions. Mother Mary's guidance can set us free, as it literally did for **Sue Tanida**, who was locked in a bathroom:

The doorknob on one of Sue's bathrooms broke, and she was trapped in a small windowless space. It took almost a half hour for someone to fix the doorknob mechanism from the outside, so she was panicking and hyperventilating and feeling like she couldn't breathe.

Sue called upon Mother Mary for help, and instantly, a soothing voice inside her head said to put her mouth near the door latch so she could feel air coming in. She did so, and the cool airflow calmed her down. She kept her head there and kept repeating the Hail Mary prayer.

Sue then heard in her head, "Move away from the door," and it's a good thing she did—the door swung open 30 seconds later. Mother Mary also prevented her from hitting her head!

Sue's rescue shows the ingenuity and power of Mother Mary to protect us in all situations. The Blessed Mother is unlimited in her ability to shine protective light upon us in our hour of need. In the following story (which has some graphic details), **Mary Webster** and her companions were saved from a harrowing scenario by Mother Mary's voice and guidance.

Mary was named after her grandmother, who was herself named after the Blessed Mother. Her Mother Mary experience occurred when she was ten years old.

It was a hot day in August of 1968. She and her cousin Ray, who was then eight, and a neighbor friend, Mark, who was five, had asked permission to go to the local city swimming pool. Up until this time, they had never been allowed to walk to the pool unaccompanied by an older sibling. After a great deal of pleading, they were permitted to go on one condition: that they *didn't* cut through the cemetery behind Mary's home (the park was located just on the other side), but rather, they had to walk the longer route, along the main road.

They agreed, and walked along the main road as instructed. They arrived at the pool very hot but happy. Mary doesn't recall the exact time they were to be home, but she does remember being exhausted from swimming, and dreading the long, hot walk back. So, the three kids decided to take the shortcut. Needless to say, she was feeling pretty guilty about being in charge of the small group and disobeying her mother. But the boys looked so tired and hot, and she was definitely feeling the same way.

As the children approached the cemetery gate, Mary saw a strange man sitting a short distance away in the gazebo, reading a newspaper. She wondered if they should turn back and travel home along the main road, as they had promised, to avoid passing by the stranger.

Just then, seemingly out of nowhere, a *different* man approached them and asked them where they were heading. Mary told him, "We're taking a shortcut home, through the cemetery."

She recalls having an uneasy feeling as she talked with him, accompanied by the thought that they should all run toward the gazebo.

The man informed them that he knew of a much shorter route, and if they would follow him behind the cemetery fence, he would show them. The boys were happy to have an even shorter walk, but Mary hesitated, as she didn't think it was a good idea. However, the man was very convincing, and although she agreed to go, she has never forgotten that urge she felt to run, or to pick up the big stick she saw along the walk to protect her charges and herself. But fear prevented her from doing either.

Once the children had reached the top of the hill, behind the cemetery, Mary realized that it wasn't shorter, after all. The man then asked if she'd like to earn some money. She said yes, thinking how nice it would be to go home with money for her parents. She asked him how. He then told her to remove her bathing-suit bottom and lie down on the ground. She was petrified, and said that no, she didn't want to earn money; she wanted to go home.

Mary didn't know anything about sexuality, but she knew that this wasn't something anyone should ask her to do. She honestly doesn't recall if the man threatened her, but she was deeply frightened and did as he said.

The man then told the boys to kneel and face the other way. They must have seen or felt Mary's fear, or known themselves that this wasn't right, and they began to cry. In her mind, Mary began to pray to the Blessed Mother for help. She sincerely believed she was about to die, and was just hoping it would be over quickly and she could go to heaven.

The man had undone his pants, and knelt in front of her. As he did so, she thought of the Blessed Mother, actually "seeing" her in all her beauty, with the sun all around her. Then she heard a voice encouraging her to "pray out loud." Mary thought that the Blessed Mother wanted her to do this because she was about to die, so she closed her eyes and tearfully began saying the Hail Mary aloud: "Hail Mary, full of grace, the Lord is with thee. Blessed art thou amongst women, and blessed is the fruit of thy womb, Jesus. Holy Mary, Mother of God, pray for us sinners now, and at the hour of our death. Amen."

At that moment, Ray stood up and started to run. Mark was still crying, and Mary thinks the man told him to go as well.

Mary prayed, and waited to die, but nothing happened. She didn't feel any pain, and there was no sound, so she slowly opened her eyes, expecting to be in heaven with the Blessed Mother. She then saw the man from the gazebo standing there staring at her. He said, "Go . . . go home . . . and remember to never talk to strangers again."

Astonished and frightened, Mary jumped up, grabbed her towel, and began running, calling out "Thank you" to the gazebo man as she ran from him, although she didn't know why.

She remembers the sun behind the trees, and the air—it wasn't hot anymore—and she kept running . . . until she saw her sister running toward her, and she knew she was safe.

When Mother Mary issues a warning, it's up to us to notice and follow her guidance. Usually, her warnings are clear and to the point, so there's no possibility of miscommunication. Mother Mary's calming presence keeps us cool while we're following her Divine guidance so that we're able to think clearly in stressful situations.

Answered Prayers of Protection

I admire people who have the presence of mind to pray for help when they're afraid or in a dangerous situation. When you're anxious, sometimes the first reaction is to curse or to say something negative. That's why the following stories inspire me, as these folks' instinctive reaction to danger was prayer. Whether they learned this from their parents, from their own solid faith, or because they were desperate for help, their prayers worked!

For example, **Philomena Chillino**'s first experience with Mother Mary was as a five-year-old girl, and the very first prayer she learned was the Hail Mary. She always felt that praying to the Blessed Mother came easy to her, and she sensed an inexplicable connection to her.

Philomena's family lived in a split-level house in Mahwah, New Jersey, and her mother, being Italian, loved to cook, so they had a freezer full of food in the cellar. Philomena's mother would frequently send her daughter down to get food out of the freezer, but she was always afraid, because every time she would go down there, she would hear voices. So normally she would cover her ears, run into the room, grab the food, and run all the way upstairs as quickly as possible.

One day when her mother sent her down to the cellar, Philomena got to the door, and the voices became very loud. They were saying, "Help me." Of course, Philomena ran back upstairs to report this to her mom, but her mother told her to just go back down and ignore the voices. So she slowly went to the door, petrified. She didn't know what to do. So Philomena prayed for help, and she then heard another voice say to her, "Don't be afraid. Just pray for them."

The only prayer Philomena knew was the Hail Mary. She slowly opened the cellar door and started to enter. As she did so, she saw human figures on all four walls. She began saying the Hail Mary, and every time she repeated the prayer, one by one, each person disappeared. From that day on, she never saw or heard the voices again.

Mother Mary also appeared to Philomena right in front of her eyes when she was in her mid-20s. Her children were young, and life was a bit difficult at that time, so she needed all the help she could get. Mary told Philomena never to feel alone, because she was always by her side.

To this day, Philomena prays for Mother Mary's help to guide her to be a better mother to her children, and now to her foster children.

☙❧

I find the outcome of Philomena's Mother Mary experiences so beautiful, because they stirred enough faith within her that her own children are now benefitting. Because of her childhood experiences, Philomena knows that the Blessed Mother is watching over her. And that knowledge is being passed along to her children, which is one of the greatest gifts we can give to our sons and daughters.

This next story is especially compelling because it occurs in South Africa, which (as I know from personal experience, having visited the country) can be a very dangerous place, especially at night:

In 1995, **Charlene Yared-West** and her mom were on their way back to Pretoria from Johannesburg (about an hour-and-a-half drive) late one afternoon after visiting a friend. It was almost sunset when their car broke down on the highway, and they were terrified. It was a time of great violence and crime in South Africa, and although Charlene was never one to complain or be negative about the state of affairs in the country, as many others were, it was scary to think that they were stranded at dusk without a cell phone between them.

They got out of the car to look for an SOS phone on the side of the road and started walking, praying the Hail Mary out loud repeatedly. Eventually they came across a phone about a mile from where their car was parked. They tried it, but it was out of order! Worried now that they were running out of options, they realized they had to do something rash. Looking across the four lanes of the highway, Charlene saw high walls that indicated the edge of a suburb. There was no way into the suburban area from the highway unless one was prepared to scale the walls or walk another 20 miles farther!

She told her mother the plan, and she said they should try, even though it was incredibly dangerous to cross a four-lane highway on foot and then scale a wall that might have electric fencing, or guard dogs on the other side (both of which are the norm in South Africa).

Praying another Hail Mary, they looked for a break in the oncoming traffic and ran across the road. On the opposite side, the grass was high and thorny. They chose a wall that had a brick face, which would be relatively easy to scale. Charlene's mother helped her up, and when she looked over the wall, there was no sign of a dog. She went right over (feeling like a thief!) and started calling to the people inside the house that was there. To her dismay, a dog came running out, quite aggressively, but luckily the owner of the house followed right behind.

A chair was passed over the wall so Charlene's mother could climb over, and then they all went inside the house, where they were given sugary tea and cookies to calm their nerves. It turned out that this woman and her husband were on the police force. They helped Charlene and her mom get their car towed, and then contacted her dad so he could pick them up.

Charlene knows that it was Mother Mary who guided them through the whole ordeal, and she and her mother will be forever grateful for her help.

Mother Mary can only intervene to the degree that we allow her to. Like God and all of heaven, she respects our freewill decisions. So, praying for help is a way to open the door for the Blessed Mother's Divine intervention, as we'll explore in the next chapter.

CHAPTER SEVEN

PRAYERS TO THE BELOVED MOTHER

While appeals for Mother Mary's help traditionally involve the Rosary and Hail Marys, there are many other ways to invoke her presence. Just as you would respond to your child's cries for help, regardless of the words he or she used, Mother Mary unconditionally comes to our aid. This includes calming away worries with her healing presence.

Caroline Cording had a wonderful experience with Mother Mary. One summer she was very afraid that she would lose her son, Tobias. He was all right, but she continually worried about his safety.

One day when Tobias was staying with his dad, Caroline prayed to Mother Mary, asking her to take care of her son while he was with his father. She then had a vision that the Blessed Mother came to her with Tobias in her arms, and there was a feeling of peace, love, and protection emanating from her.

The relief that Caroline felt was so strong that she could take a deep breath and finally let go of her fears about her son. It was very beautiful—a sensation she'll never forget!

Who among us doesn't worry occasionally? But sometimes, these anxieties become chronic and erode peace of mind, as was the case for Caroline. How beautiful that she discovered the "cure" for worrying through prayer for Mother Mary's assistance.

Mother Mary comes to us, regardless of how we appeal for her help. As an unconditionally loving parent, she responds to all varieties of prayer. While "Hail Mary" is the traditional Catholic petition to request Mother Mary's intercession, the Blessed Mother also helps those who pray in different ways. **Rita-Marie Lenton**'s story is a perfect example:

The blessed Virgin Mary has always been a huge influence on Rita-Marie's life, as she was raised Catholic, and attended a Catholic school in her hometown of Winton, Queensland, Australia. She stopped attending church, however, when she sought out a priest to help her deal with the sexual abuse that was being perpetrated upon her by her stepfather. Instead of helping her, he told her that she was a sinner, and that she had to repent for her sins by saying ten Our Fathers and ten Hail Marys.

Lucky for her, Mother Mary had already taught Rita-Marie that she *wasn't* a sinner. In fact, Mary was the one she turned to every time she had difficulties in her life, and she would often feel Mary's loving hands around her. It was the Blessed Mother who taught Rita-Marie how to live through the trauma of sexual abuse, and how to detach herself from her body so that she wouldn't feel the pain. Mother Mary also taught her how to work on forgiving the perpetrator (but not condoning the act) as a way of healing herself.

These days, if Rita-Marie is feeling down or distressed, she recites the Hail Mary, slightly changing the prayer to:

"Hail Mary, full of Grace, the Lord is with thee.
Blessed art thou amongst women, and blessed is the fruit
of thy womb, Jesus. Holy Mary, Mother of God, pray
for us now, and at the hour of our death. Amen."

She leaves out the word *sinners,* as Mary often told her when she was a young girl that *none of us* are sinners.

Now a funeral director, Rita-Marie meets with and consoles many families, and she always asks Mary to help them during their time of need.

I just love this story, because it shows the beautiful ripple effect of Mother Mary's love, with Rita-Marie praying that the Beloved Mother help other people. These prayers are immediately effective in various ways, often unexpected. And as **Stephen Mascovich** discovered, saying prayers for Mother Mary also brings about inner peace:

About 12 years ago, Stephen started praying the Rosary every day. There were a few stressful situations in his life at that time, and he remembered from his early years that saying the Rosary could be beneficial.

He experienced an immediate lessening of his stress, although the circumstances he was concerned about were still present. However, he felt much better able to cope with everything, both emotionally and physically. On days when he was feeling particularly stressed, he prayed the Rosary multiple times.

Stephen also noticed that if he found himself awake at night and couldn't fall back to sleep, saying a Hail Mary would soon make him sleepy. And these days, he also prays to Mother Mary when he anticipates being involved in difficult situations, which helps him immensely.

As Stephen discovered, just the act of praying brings relief from anxiety and stress. As soon as you pray, you can sense Mother Mary's involvement. The weight of worry is lifted from you, as she reassures your mind and heart that all is well. Then she answers your prayers in undreamed-of ways.

Prayers for a Soul Mate

Mother Mary loves family life, and she desires our happiness. So it makes sense that she'll happily introduce us to the partner with whom we'll share the joys of marriage and parenting.

Kristin Marie Rodriguez always felt that Mother Mary had such a kind, sweet, and loving energy. She grew up Catholic and would always pray to the Blessed Mother. She can remember her first prayer to her, at the age of 16. She lit a white candle with an image of Our Lady nearby, and said a prayer requesting that she find her true love, her soul mate, during that time.

Now that she thinks about it 12 years later, it may have been silly to ask for love at such a young age, but her wish was granted. A few months after she uttered that prayer, Kristin met her soul mate, who is now her husband.

Kristin strongly believes that Mother Mary helped her meet her soul mate at just the right time, and that they were meant to be in each other's lives. What a blessing!

Undoubtedly, Mother Mary gave Kristin guidance that led her to her soul mate. Fortunately, Kristin was smart enough to hear and follow that inner guidance (which usually appears as intuitive feelings or urges to take action steps).

In the next story, Mother Mary appeared in a night-time vision that literally led a woman to find her "dream husband":

Vicky Flores is Mexican, and was raised in a Catholic family. When she was 16, she met a young man and fell head over heels in love with him. Her parents didn't like him at all, though, so it really was a very difficult relationship, as in Mexico daughters typically live with their parents until they get married.

Anyway, six years later, Vicky and her boyfriend got married in a Catholic church, but they went on to follow their own traditions. In fact, they felt so separated from the laws of the Church and spirituality that Vicky and her husband didn't even really believe in God's existence anymore. Four years later, the couple decided to get a divorce. She felt totally alone and cried every day. Her heart was completely broken, so she started praying during her walk to work, apologizing to God for having forsaken Him for so long.

One night in a dream, Vicky saw the image of Mother Mary, who told her that she was bringing her a "real gentleman." Three years later, she met a wonderful man, and against her family's traditions and again without her parents' consent, she accepted his proposal. Vicky knew in her heart that she had really done everything she could have to save her first marriage, but to no avail. So she talked to God, and she believed that He didn't think she was doing anything wrong by remarrying. However, the Catholic Church doesn't allow second marriages, and of course, she was doing something against her family's will. But nevertheless, she did get married to this wonderful man.

Then Vicky submitted her case to the archbishop's office, requesting an annulment of her first marriage. The entire process ended up taking seven years!

In February 2000, Vicky was participating in a prayer circle and was asked if she would like to keep an image of Mother Mary in her home. It was a picture that the different members of the circle shared with each other. Vicky said yes without hesitation, and when she saw the image, she realized it was the exact same one she'd seen in her dream ten years previously. At that moment, she knew that Mother Mary was taking care of her situation.

In Mexico, Mother's Day is celebrated on May 10, and it was on that precise day that Vicky received a letter from the archbishop's office declaring her first marriage annulled. The letter was postmarked April 30 (Children's Day), and Vicky knew that this was Mother Mary's doing, as the Blessed Mother considered Vicky to be her child.

Vicky and her husband were so happy, and immediately began preparations to make their current marriage legal under the Church's rules. They didn't want to have any type of special celebration, though, because for Vicky and her husband, their first wedding date was the one they would acknowledge; but since the Church required them to go through a certain process, they did so.

Finally, everything was arranged, and the priest asked Vicky and her husband to take their marriage vows in a formal service just to have Church requirements met. They agreed to do so the following Friday.

When she realized that the date of that Friday was September 8, Vicky was certain that Mother Mary had played a part in all this. September 8 is the day that the Catholic Church celebrates the Blessed Mother's birthday!

To this day, Mother Mary is a very important part of Vicky and her husband's lives . . . and will be as long as they love and live!

Whether you're praying for relationships, health, or other life issues, Mother Mary answers each appeal with compassion and support.

In the Appendix of this book, you'll find some traditional and also modern Mother Mary prayers. In the next chapter, you'll learn how she helps with our work and life purpose.

CHAPTER EIGHT

PURPOSEFUL CAREERS AND ABUNDANT SUPPLY

Like any loving parent, Mother Mary wants all of God's children (us) to have their needs met. Just as you'd want *your* children to be happy, so it is for Mother Mary!

So, it's no surprise that people have had prayers answered in those areas of life that affect happiness, including a satisfying career, or just earning enough money to pay the bills.

For many people, getting a job isn't enough. They want a career that brings them a sense of meaning and purpose, and Mother Mary's wisdom can steer them in the right direction.

Growing up in a Catholic home, **Kristy M. Ayala** was exposed to images and stories about Mother Mary on a regular basis. Even as a young child, she had a strong fascination with the Blessed Mother, and would often stare at her statue during Mass. She felt connected to the sensation of love that she felt as she looked upon Mary's face.

Throughout her childhood and even as she got older and moved away from home, Kristy maintained that adoration for Mother Mary and that special place for her in her heart. But it wasn't until she was in college that she really began to work with the Blessed Mother more regularly, and in a more personal way.

Kristy began asking Our Lady to be with her and to guide her as she moved through her daily life. She could genuinely feel a great sense of love and peace in her heart when she would ask Mary to help her, as well as a loving and motherly feeling within her in response to her requests for support. Being 500 miles away from her closest family member from the time she was 18, Kristy derived a great deal of comfort from this.

As she moved through college and graduate school, and throughout her coursework in psychology, she continued to foster her relationship with the Blessed Mother. Kristy had many different types of jobs during those years, but there was a time when she wasn't working for about nine months, which was very challenging for her. She felt frustrated and didn't understand why she couldn't get hired, even for jobs for which she was overqualified.

She finally surrendered, making peace with the fact that she now had more free time. Kristy began to work on some personal projects and was truly feeling happy and loving, and she told herself that when the right job came along, she would know it and be able to transition into it easily. She told herself that she didn't need to fight or push to find the right job. She realized that all of the employment opportunities she'd had in the past were smooth transitions, and that this would be, too.

Then Kristy interviewed for a position that a very good friend had recommended her for, and even though it wasn't exactly the direction she had planned to take as the next step in her career, she was hired on the spot. So she thought, *Well, there must be a good reason why I got this job.*

The position allowed her to do work that she had never expected to do, involving child advocacy and direct intervention work. When the time came for her to move on, she felt that she was ushered just as easily and smoothly into her next position, which allowed her to teach psychology at a university. This led her to combine her background in psychology with her Angel Therapy® practice.

Over the years since beginning her private practice, Kristy has noticed that many of her clients have a connection with Mother Mary. This made her realize that Mary has been with her all along—helping her shape and build the career that would put her exactly where she needed to be. It was only a few years ago that she read that Mother Mary works closely with child advocates, educators, parents, and healers.

Kristy now realizes that Mother Mary has guided her to all of the jobs she's had where she is helping young people— whether they are newborns, teens, or college age. And she also sees that Mary continues to support her in her healing practice by bringing her just the right clients.

Although she is not a parent, Kristy has been able to be a support system for parents along the way as well. She feels so grateful and so blessed to have the love and assistance of Mother Mary, who has guided her to go where she is needed, and to do the work that she is destined for as she continues on her path.

You can pray for Mother Mary's help anywhere and in any way, and receive her powerful guidance. I have found, however, that when I enter a church dedicated to Mother Mary, I feel an even stronger connection with her. It's not that it's necessary to address her in her sanctuaries. Rather, it's the effect of lighting white candles among others, and the years of many people praying within the walls of the church. This helps me focus my prayers with more clarity. A woman named **Mely** had just such an experience:

Mely had earned a master's degree in criminal justice, but she had been unemployed for over a year. As a result, every few months she had to call her student-loan lenders to apply for an unemployment deferment on her accounts, as she couldn't make the payments. She still lived with her parents, and they were helping her out while she continued with her job search.

On one particular day, Mely asked her parents to take her to the Basilica of the National Shrine of the Immaculate Conception in Washington, D.C. She wanted to talk to the Blessed Mother and pray for her help.

Her parents granted her request, and Mely poured her heart out in front of a mural of Mother Mary. She asked her to help her find a job, and to provide guidance with her finances. Mely knew in her heart that her life purpose was to help people, and her career goal was to be in the law-enforcement realm. Afterward, she lit a candle at the church and asked Mother Mary to send her a sign that she would help her.

Mely then went looking for her mother so that they could go home. As she and her parents were exiting the church, she felt guided to enter another room that had a different mural of blessed Mother Mary, where she was clutching some rosary beads in her hand and holding baby Jesus on her lap. Mely went inside the room to find a beautiful pink rose on top of the table that was in front of the mural. At that moment, she felt in her heart that Mary was guiding her in the right direction.

A few days after her visit, Mely got a call from a law-enforcement agency that she had applied to a few months before. The recruiter asked her if she was still interested in the job, and if she wanted to come in for an interview. Of course she said yes. Words cannot adequately express the hope and joy Mely has in her heart. What a blessing!

❧

What would you do if your adult children called you and asked you for food? Naturally you'd help them as best as you could. Well, that's how Mother Mary responds to prayers to provide us with enough to eat. These prayers are often answered in unusual and unexpected ways, as a woman named **Lisa** discovered:

Lisa's mom had gotten laid off from both of her jobs, there was hardly any food in the house, and Lisa wasn't sure what to think anymore. She had believed in angels, God, and ascended masters for so long, but now it seemed that none of it existed or really meant anything. Lisa was in a dark place, and didn't have a clue how anything could turn around or if things would just continue to get worse.

In desperation, Lisa pulled out my book *Archangels & Ascended Masters* and asked out loud who might be with her whom she could work with. She opened up the book right to the "Mary, the Beloved Mother" page. She reread who Mary was and what she could assist with, and took comfort in the true stories of others who had been helped by the Blessed Mother.

Lisa used the method of invoking Mother Mary that I suggested, and also put out an SOS to Mary, asking her if she could provide her with physical evidence of her presence. But Lisa really wasn't expecting a response, because she had such a lack of faith at that time.

The next day, Lisa's mom exclaimed that the money she had been waiting for had appeared in her account. She was so shocked that she asked a bank employee to check to make sure it was the correct account number and truly belonged to her, since it was nothing short of a miracle.

Then, that weekend, Lisa's grandma visited and gave her a gift, saying, "Lisa, I want you to have this, since it's very old and I don't want it anymore." Little did Grandma know why she had been compelled to bring the gift to her grand-daughter: it was a statue of Mary holding Jesus, and it featured her in the role of the compassionate mother!

Lisa almost couldn't believe her eyes, but she decided to accept the wondrous events that were occurring and just express gratitude to the Blessed Mother!

In dire circumstances, Mother Mary's compassion comes shining through like a lighthouse illuminating our passage to smoother sailing and a safe harbor. Desperate for help, **Sue Schaffer** appealed to the Blessed Mother:

Since early childhood, Sue has been very strongly connected with the Blessed Mother. She was raised Roman Catholic, so praying the Rosary was a big part of her life. She never fully understood the way the church had her say the Rosary, though, so she just did it her own way. She would go through each section of ten beads, saying the Hail Mary while focusing on what it was she wanted for herself or another. And it always worked.

The miracle that occurred relating to the Blessed Mother is from a period in Sue's life when she (a single mother) and her four children were homeless. They had been evicted from their house in 1996, and for the next year and a half, they lived in a motel that Sue paid for by working as much as she could.

But the cost of living in the motel left little to save, so finding suitable housing was crucial. At one point, Sue really began to lose hope. That's when she decided to pray to a Blessed Mother statue at a nearby church. She also began bringing her flowers, as she had heard that Mother Mary liked them. During this period, Sue was given an emergency Section 8 voucher to help pay for housing, and she found the home that she's now lived in for 14 years.

From the time she started praying, it took approximately six weeks for all of this to unfold. Sue knows in her heart of hearts that her connection to Mother Mary is what fueled the miracle. She believes that the Blessed Mother sits next to her bed and watches over her family . . . and that she always will.

How beautiful that Sue and her family now have a permanent home, thanks to Mother Mary's Divine intervention. Every detail of a stressful situation can be referred to the Blessed Mother, in the same way you'd discuss your troubles with a loving and compassionate parent. This is true in the case of trying to make difficult decisions, too:

A friend of **Franka Tiralongo**'s brought the Community Association for Riding for the Disabled (CARD)—a place that provides therapeutic horseback riding for children and adults with special needs—to her attention one day, and she was considering doing volunteer work there. Franka had a child who was developmentally delayed and had autistic tendencies, so she felt it was her purpose to work with these children.

In a short amount of time, Franka had encountered three individuals who were volunteers at CARD, and by the time she ran into the third one, she had chills running up and down her body, but she was contemplating whether she should put in an application at other places where she could volunteer in order to keep her options open. She was praying for guidance to help her make a decision.

One morning just before she woke up, Franka had a dream that she was at Holland Bloorview Kids Rehabilitation Hospital in Toronto, Canada, and she was in a meeting with a woman who was volunteering there. She looked out the window and saw her daughter in her backyard at home by herself, so she ran outside to be with her, finding her at the end of the yard where the fence divided her property from that of the neighbors who lived behind her.

Suddenly, in the spot where she was standing, the fence was no longer there and the backyard expanded into a beautiful park. Franka came upon a path made out of colorful mosaic tiles, and she walked until it parted in two different directions. Just before the fork, there was a picture of Mother Mary holding baby Jesus right on the mosaic-tiled path. Franka then found herself back at the house, and the gate was open about two to three inches.

This dream was very meaningful to Franka. The woman in her dream was her Slovenian second-grade teacher, and after 26 years, she'd run into her at the Bloorview hospital just a few months before she'd had this dream. Franka mentioned to her that she was a lawyer and was making a career change to work with children with special needs, and volunteering at Bloorview in the process. Interestingly enough, the teacher's name was Maria.

Anyway, Franka realized that Mother Mary was guiding her to another opportunity. She had some health challenges she was recovering from, and she chose CARD because she wanted to be around horses, as they have powerful healing effects on people. She realized that this is why she was guided in that direction in the first place. With her love for and connection to animals and children, she was happy to be of service to them.

Mother Mary helped Franka decide to work with horses, which of course turned out to be the choice that brought her the most meaning and happiness. The Blessed Mother is especially adept at opening us up to occupations that will ultimately help the children of the world. If you feel passionate about working with young people, be sure to ask Mother Mary for assistance with your career.

Many times, Mother Mary answers prayers by giving us signs and visions, which is a topic we'll explore in more detail in the next chapter.

CHAPTER NINE

SIGNS FROM MOTHER MARY

We've all seen news accounts of people seeing the shape of Mother Mary in unusual locations, such as on toasted bread or reflected on windows. Believers call this phenomenon *acheiropoieta,* which describes religious icons that are Divinely created without human hands. Some of them are recognized as miracles by the Catholic Church.

The term *simulacra* refers to *perceptions* of religious icons within natural objects. Most scientists believe that our minds are wired to see patterns of human faces amid random images. Yet, if it happens to you, *your* mind may be changed. You may be convinced that Mother Mary has the power to affect material objects so that we know she's watching over us all.

Here's a remarkable example from a woman who saw the shape of Mother Mary in ordinary tissues:

For years **Maria Hardi** had been looking for a large statue of the Virgin Mary. She finally found one and put her it in one of the rooms in her home. She even painted the wall behind the statue so that it would stand out.

A couple of weeks later, the family pet, Omlette, passed away, and Maria and her eight-year-old daughter, Lili, were naturally very upset. Maria tried to comfort Lili by telling her that Omlette was now in heaven, and Mother Mary and the angels were looking after him.

Maria then walked into the bathroom and saw that the tissues in the box were standing up straight and arranged in perfect shape of the Virgin Mary!

Maria called Lili into the bathroom and asked her if the tissues looked like anything, and right away her young daughter put her hand over her mouth in disbelief and exclaimed, "Mary!"

They both acknowledged that a tissue couldn't have stood up like that on its own. This lasted for two days, and provided Maria and her daughter with the comfort they needed.

სა

Although tissues shaped like the Madonna may sound silly, for Maria and Lili it was comforting confirmation. These signs are personal, and come to us in unique and individualized ways. Sometimes, the signs are crystal clear, such as when Mother Mary shows you an image of herself:

Carly had been going through some big changes in her life: she was living in a part of the world (Canberra, Australia) where she had no family, and then she lost her job.

About a week before, she had reported a co-worker for making repeated sexual comments to both her and the receptionist at the company where she worked. She decided to finally say something about it when this man came up behind her one day and put his hands on her hips and would not let go. Carly had to pry them off.

To her surprise, instead of helping her, her manager, who was new to the position, laid Carly off. She was given a piece of paper saying that that would be her last day. Carly was in complete shock, because she had been with the company for two years and loved her job.

She went back to her desk and quietly packed up her things and walked out. She didn't know what to say, and didn't want to start crying, so she didn't even get the chance to tell anyone what had happened and say good-bye.

Before Carly left, though, she sent an e-mail to a friend whom she had been e-mailing back and forth with throughout the day. She told him not to bother replying to her work e-mail again because she no longer worked there. When Carly got home, she discovered that her friend had e-mailed her to ask if she would be interested in a job at the company where *he* worked—which was at a significantly higher wage and *fitted* her skill set perfectly. She wrote back right away to say she'd definitely be interested, and sent him her résumé.

Interestingly enough, about a week or so before she was laid off, Carly had changed her desktop computer background to a picture of Mother Mary holding the baby Jesus. This image brought her great comfort, so she wanted it in a place where she would see it often. She had been going through a tough time because a romantic relationship had just ended, and on the days when she was really struggling with the pain, she would look at the picture on her computer and pretend that she was Jesus and that Mary was her mother. The way he was resting in the Blessed Mother's arms just looked so peaceful, and Carly wished that she had someone in *her* life whom she could lean on in that way.

Then, a few days later, she turned on her iPod and noticed that the little "lock" screen had changed to a picture of Mother Mary! She had no idea how this could have happened, but it was definitive proof that the Blessed Mother was always with her, helping her in every way.

Likewise, **Mary Theresa** always sensed that Mother Mary was by her side as she went about her life. On one particular day, Mary Theresa felt that she really needed to get a tangible sign that Mother Mary was truly with her. She asked for some form of assurance, and then released the request to the universe, knowing in her heart that she would receive what she needed.

Anyway, Mary Theresa was shopping and doing other errands later that day, and when she was getting in her car at one point, she saw something on the ground by the driver's side of her automobile. As she came closer and picked it up, she could see that it was a sleeve cover from a music CD with Mother Mary's picture on the front! Mary Theresa shivered all over, and beamed inside and out. She knew beyond any shadow of a doubt that Mother Mary was with her . . . and she felt so blessed.

Sometimes, Mother Mary guides other people to bring signs to us. Even though these signs aren't appearing mysteriously from out of nowhere, they're powerful indicators of her presence nonetheless. Such was the case in the following unusual string of events involving Oreo cookies and the Blessed Mother:

Mother Mary has become a very prominent part of **Donna T.**'s life, and her story begins with a dream. In it, Donna was at a hospital that was overloaded with injured and ill patients. There was one huge room crowded with people lying on cots all crammed together. Donna seemed to be on some kind of a tour. There were a few other people with her, and they were all following a couple of doctors, who were having a discussion or teaching. As they all walked along, Donna stopped hearing what the doctors were saying and instead began noticing the suffering the surrounding people were enduring.

As she walked, the patients would hold their arms out, crying for help. Donna felt so much empathy for them and realized that the doctors seemed oblivious to their pain. She knew somehow that some of these people had been in the hospital for months and weren't getting any better.

Suddenly, Donna realized she had something that could be of help to them. She was wearing a fanny pack and decided that she couldn't keep what she had in there hidden any longer. Maybe she could help these people who were in need. She knew she had to try. So she opened the pack and inside were Oreo cookies. Yes, Oreo cookies were her simple medicine! She handed a cookie to one person and told him it was okay to eat it, that he would feel better as a result. He couldn't walk; in fact, he looked as if he had been in battle and was in extreme pain. In an instant, though, he transformed as he ate the cookie. He smiled, thanked her, got up, and actually ran out of the building.

Donna was a bit stunned, but so happy. She handed an Oreo cookie to another person, and the same thing happened. So she began to give cookies to each person she walked past. More people were reaching for cookies, yet they were trying to be quiet and not call attention to what was happening. She kept handing out the cookies.

As she handed out the last one, she bumped into someone. She looked up and it was one of the doctors. He was huge, and towered over her. He mumbled some words, then yelled at her, "You can't do this! Who do you think you are?!" He went on to tell her that *they* knew what to do, and she was hurting the patients by giving them false hope. Also, this was not allowed. Donna pointed out that the patients were responding and healing, and it was a good thing. But he told her she had to stop. She was confused and began to feel a little intimidated.

Then the doctor glanced down at the open fanny pack, which was now empty. He looked at Donna and said, "Well, you're out of cookies anyway, and there is nothing that can help these people, so it's over; it has to be done our way."

Donna looked up at him and suddenly felt this energy surge within her and an inner strength. She closed the fanny pack, and as she looked directly into the doctor's eyes, she very calmly said, "No, Mother Mary will always provide for them." She opened the fanny pack and it was full of Oreo cookies again.

The doctor was shocked, but Donna was calm, and she woke up from the dream right then. She had an incredibly wonderful feeling when she did so, and knew that Mary was with her and that there was so much meaning in the dream for her. She wrote down the details and her thoughts right away.

A few days later, Donna was traveling with a couple of friends. They were heading out to a weekend workshop, which was about a four-hour drive away. As they were driving, they began to talk about dreams, so Donna decided to share hers. Her friends agreed that it was wonderful and full of meaning. When they got to the retreat center where the workshop was being held, they all went off in different directions to find their rooms and prepare for the evening class.

Donna decided to take a walk on the beautiful grounds before the class began. Awhile later, as she was walking back toward the classroom, she stopped under a beautiful tree. She looked up into it and began to talk to Mary. She told her she appreciated the dream and the message. However, she needed a sign. She asked Mary to please give her something to prove that she had really spoken to her through the dream, and that she was truly with her. Donna then felt a beautiful presence around her, and for a moment, everything seemed surreal. She was enjoying the experience, but then noticed the time. She thanked Mary and headed off to class.

Once the class was over, Donna chatted with people for a while, then went off to her room. But when she opened the door, something seemed different. There were two small beds, and she was staying in the room alone. She noticed that the pillow on the bed she wasn't going to use had been moved and was now sitting on top of the pillow that was on the bed she *was* going to sleep in. She knew she hadn't moved it when she had been there earlier.

The items she had unpacked were where she had left them. It was just the pillows that were different. Donna stood there for a moment wondering what was going on, then walked over to the bed. As she slowly lifted the top pillow, she saw something shiny sticking out from beneath the other one below it. As she moved the bottom pillow, she gasped. There were two packages of Oreo cookies under the pillows!

Mother Mary had granted her request for a sign! The next morning, Donna told her friends what had happened and asked them if they'd put the cookies there. At first they acted as if they didn't know anything, but they finally admitted that they'd put the cookies there.

As they talked about it, they realized that at the very moment Donna was out by the tree and everything seemed to become surreal, her two friends had been in a store, and one of them had felt compelled to buy Oreo cookies for Donna in light of her dream. When they returned from the store, they also then felt compelled to put them in her room and hide them instead of just giving them to her. They were stunned when she told them how she had talked to Mary and had asked for a sign.

Donna has no doubt that Mother Mary granted her request . . . and will always be by her side.

❦

A skeptic could dismiss Mary's story because her friends knew of her Oreo dream. Still, I believe her observation that her friends' timing in being guided to buy and hide the Oreos was remarkable. Heaven works in unusual ways, after all!

Here's another story where someone else's actions brought Mother Mary's comfort to a person in need:

Helping others is something **Melanie Orders** has always done, but one day, feeling very down and uninspired about her life, she prayed for some guidance. She asked God, Jesus, Mother Mary, and Archangel Michael to let her know they were with her; and to give her a sign that she should continue on her path.

A few days later, her youngest daughter, Lilli, came home from school and said she had been given a necklace by a nun who had been delivering a speech at her school. Melanie thought that this was very nice and asked if she could have a look at it. Lilli said yes, and then said, "Mummy, you can have it—I don't want to wear it."

Melanie thanked her daughter, and then looked at the necklace closely. She could see the image of Mother Mary on one side of the pendant. Tears welled up in her eyes, as she had been given a beautiful heavenly sign that she was indeed looked after, and that her prayers were being heard and answered.

Melanie carries the pendant with her in her handbag, as the chain is now broken. It is in a pouch she holds when she feels alone, or has lost her faith or direction.

Signs can also come as feelings. You may get a strong and unmistakable sense or knowingness that Mother Mary is with you or is helping you. **Ekaterina** has had that feeling of being in Mary's presence several times, and the experience was always very delicate and gentle.

The first time Ekaterina encountered the Blessed Mother, she saw her light in the form of a white shiny shape in a long dress. At that time, she was praying to her, but she didn't expect to have that special feeling of her presence, and of course, she didn't expect to see her. Ekaterina was very grateful for that experience, as she felt that it was such a huge sign of God's mercy, as well as the fact that Mother Mary had heard her prayers.

In subsequent experiences, Ekaterina didn't actually *see* Mother Mary, but *sensed* her presence beside or in front of her. But in those cases, she remembered the way she'd felt while in her presence in the past, so she knew that it was Mother Mary again. Sometimes she wondered if there was something within her that didn't permit her to completely connect to Mary. At those times, she prayed, asking that any blocks to the connection be removed so that she and Mother Mary could be *one.*

Now, whenever Ekaterina doubts that it's possible to "feel" Mary, she believes that it's a sign that she needs to focus her prayers to clear up the space between them.

In my experience, the feelings and sensations that Ekaterina describes are just as valid and valuable as having a full-on vision. After all, your body is extremely sensitive to changes in temperature, pressure, and magnetic and electrical levels. So it feels and recognizes strong spiritual presences, such as Mother Mary.

These signs from Mother Mary are her way of reassuring us and easing our minds, especially when we feel lonely, misunderstood, afraid, or otherwise vulnerable. In the next couple of chapters, we'll explore two very common signs from the Blessed Mother: statues and roses.

CHAPTER TEN

MOTHER MARY STATUES

When I visited Lourdes, France, the first thing I noticed before arriving at the basilica and grotto were vendors in small wooden booths, selling every conceivable product printed with images of Mother Mary. I saw Mother Mary clocks, bookmarks, wall plaques, drinking glasses, water bottles, and hundreds of statues. They even sold large glow-in-the-dark plastic rosaries.

Statues of Mother Mary and other religious icons are visual reminders of the presence of those who watch over us. They prompt us to pray, to release worries and fears, and to ask for help with whatever is bothering us.

This chapter is filled with stories of people who received messages and signs from Mother Mary through experiences with statues. This is not a new phenomenon. The Catholic Church and spiritual researchers have studied reports of "weeping statues" for decades. One especially notable case occurred in Akita, Japan, in the 1970s, and became officially recognized. There, the weeping "Our Lady of Akita" statue was visible to everyone who saw her, including those who viewed films of the statue on television.

Researchers regularly test the liquids that are reportedly tears coming from the statues, and usually find them to be human tears. But—barring someone trying to perpetuate a hoax upon the public—when an individual has a comforting vision of a crying statue, does it really matter if there is actual liquid coming from the statue's eyes?

In **Rita King**'s case, her mother found great peace when she had a vision of a weeping Mother Mary statue:

Rita's mother, who is now deceased, was very devoted to the Virgin Mary. Rita grew up Catholic, with a father who was emotionally abusive to the family. The emotional abuse was particularly difficult on Rita's mom, who was raising four willful children, without much help from her husband.

During a particularly difficult period, Rita's mom went to an empty church during the day to seek peace and refuge. She knelt right up front, at the altar, near a statue of Our Lady, and asked for help in dealing with the problems at home. Crying, she saw the statue of Our Lady move and weep, and then she received a personal message from Mother Mary that she didn't share with anyone.

Many years later, near the time of her death, she asked Rita to find a statue of the Virgin Mary. She described what she wanted in great detail. Rita was able to find exactly what she asked for: it was a very large and beautiful statue a few feet tall. Mary was wearing a beautiful blue robe, and she was standing on a serpent. Rita's mom loved it.

Her mother passed away shortly after that, and she was buried in the town where she was born. Rita carried the statue with her out of town and told the priest of her mom's devotion to Mary. He incorporated the story of the statue, and Rita's mother's devotion to Mother Mary, into the service.

Rita has the statue with her to this day, and it is very precious to her.

Dreams of Statues

Many of the Virgin Mary statue stories reported to me involved visions during dream time, such as this one from a woman named **Marguerite:**

Marguerite has always found strength, comfort, and power through her connection with the Blessed Mother.

In 2004, while living in Brooklyn during college, Marguerite decided to start praying to the Virgin Mary on her daily subway ride back home. After doing so one day, she got off at her stop and was walking up the stairs to the street level. As she placed her foot on one of the stairs, she saw something float past her face, and looking down to her feet, she saw that it was a red rose petal. She walked up the subway stairs and searched for a person selling flowers or carrying a bouquet, but found no one. She believes that Mary was just letting her know she was hearing her prayers.

In her third year of college, Marguerite was battling severe anxiety and on-and-off depression. She had been dealing with this condition since she was 16 years old, but at this time she was suffering from panic attacks pretty regularly. One night as she was falling asleep, she had a flashback of being a freshman in college and being raped by her boyfriend at the time. At first she thought it was a nightmare, but then realized she was actually still awake and that more and more memories were coming back to her. She was very startled and scared and quickly realized that these were actual memories that she had somehow forgotten or repressed.

The next day, Marguerite called the ex-boyfriend to confront him. She told him she remembered him forcing himself on her after she had said no. He told her how sorry he was. At that point, she knew for sure that all this had occurred, and that her mind had protected her from the experience by shielding her from the memory of that night. She then called some friends, and they all nonchalantly affirmed that yes, she had told them what had happened, but they didn't know what to do, so they did nothing. She was devastated, and felt helpless and alone.

That week Marguerite went to the therapy services at her college and began talking with a wonderful counselor. Also that week, the Virgin Mary appeared to her one morning. She was woken up around 7 by someone sweetly saying her name. Marguerite opened her eyes to find a life-size statue of the Virgin Mary next to her bed. She appeared to be plaster, and was in her usual blue gown, with her head tilted down a little.

Marguerite was startled to see the statue and didn't understand what was going on, but at the same time, she was completely at peace. Although she doesn't recall the lips of the statue moving, she heard a voice saying that, yes, it was Mother Mary who was with her and that she was doing fine. Mary comforted Marguerite and gave her strength. She then fell back to sleep and woke up with a strong sense of calm.

Marguerite doesn't know why Mother Mary chose to appear to her as a statue. Perhaps it was because she had a very similar statue in her bedroom at the time. Whatever the reason, Marguerite knows that Mary was letting her know that she would survive this trauma and that it would only make her stronger. After dealing with the rape and her feelings around the event, her anxiety did lessen, and she is now free of depression.

Those who'd be skeptical of Marguerite's experience and say that it was "just a dream" could focus instead upon the remarkable healing that occurred. Marguerite's freedom from depression is a beautiful testament to the healing power of dreams.

By the same token, here's what happened to a woman by the name of **Maya:**

Mother Mary came to Maya as she was taking an afternoon nap. She recalled afterward that in that dream, a statue of Mother Mary came to life, and she was sending Maya waves of energizing love and light. When she woke up, Maya felt refreshed and rejuvenated, and so very blessed to have had that experience. Maya knows that Mother Mary is always with her and that she just needs to call upon her to have her assistance.

Statues as Signs from Above

Statues of the Virgin Mary and other religious icons carry a great significance, especially if they're given to you at just the right time:

Maria M. Nguyen had been going through a very hard time, having just separated from her husband. She was feeling completely lost and heartbroken. Having always felt Mother Mary's comforting presence and healing love, she prayed to her for guidance, and asked her to show her a sign that she was with her.

The next day when picking up her children from Catholic school, Maria saw that the parking lot was full, and the only remaining spot was near several statues. After getting out of the car, she started chatting with some people affiliated with the Church who were gathered around a beautiful statue of Mother Mary. Maria commented that she had always wanted such a statue. She was then asked if she would like to bring it home. She was shocked. She couldn't believe that she had just been offered this beautiful statue of Mother Mary! What more convincing sign could she have received of her presence?

When I visited Loreto Cathedral, I was mesmerized by the Madonna statue illuminated above the Holy Home within the basilica. As I mentioned in the Introduction, all those centuries of prayer within the Holy Home made my experience feel even more profound, as I realized that my prayers were connected with countless other souls who'd prayed there previously. And the statue of the Immaculate Conception within the walls of the grotto at Lourdes was angelic in its purity and beauty. So statues can definitely serve as vessels and vehicles of prayers and healing.

In the next chapter, we'll explore the topic of roses, which are symbolic of Mother Mary.

CHAPTER ELEVEN

ROSES FROM HEAVEN

Mother Mary is often called "Our Lady of the Roses" because these beautiful flowers are one of her symbols. When we're in her sacred presence, we may smell the fragrance of roses without having any physical flowers nearby.

In fact, the name *Rosary* means "a garland of roses." The rose is considered the queen of flowers, and white ones symbolize Mother Mary. Red blooms are said to have blushed when she kissed them in heaven. In the Middle Ages, roses were used in purification ceremonies, and Mother Mary is the ultimate symbol of purity. White roses are associated with Mary's joys, red with her suffering, and yellow with her glory.

Roses are also a symbol of Saint Thérèse, the "Little Flower," so the scent or sight of roses can also signal that prayers to this saint were heard and answered. Many devotees believe that roses indicate that both Saint Thérèse *and* Mother Mary are present.

According to a beautiful story, Mother Mary appeared to Saint Juan Diego in the 1530s. No one believed him, so the Blessed Mother appointed Diego to gather roses to prove her presence to the bishop, because it was then the middle of winter when roses normally are dormant. When Diego climbed a hilltop in search of roses, he found them blooming abundantly, and his vision was believed.

Many Gothic cathedrals feature round stained-glass windows representing roses. These windows are called the

Mystical Rose, with four petals—representing the Holy Trinity, plus Mary, for a total of four.

Some theologians draw a parallel between Mother Mary's roses and the Buddhist deity Quan Yin, who is normally shown with a lotus flower. Since Quan Yin is a virgin "goddess of compassion" who's frequently called the "Mother Mary of the East," these are interesting theories.

The Fragrance of Roses

As mentioned earlier, it's fairly common for people who pray to Mother Mary to report smelling roses (even though no flowers are present). Rose fragrance is the Blessed Mother's sign to us of her presence, as **Bianca Pursley** discovered:

Bianca has been able to see things others can't from a very young age. She has always been adept at communicating with relatives on the Other Side, angels, fairies, and other beings. During her teenage years, though, the things she saw started to become very frightening. She constantly had alarming visions and saw angry spirits. As a result, she fell into a very dark place and became depressed.

One day Bianca was in her room crying and feeling hopeless, wondering if she'd ever be normal or happy, when she detected the scent of roses. She looked up and saw a vision of Mother Mary! She was so beautiful, with a bright aura of white, yellow, and pink light, and a soft, sweet smile. Bianca was instantly filled with an overwhelming sense of security and love. She felt the most comforting motherly energy embracing her, letting her know that everything was going to be okay, and that she was special and loved.

After that day, things started to look up. She met positive, spiritual people who helped her learn to control and use her abilities; and her visions stopped being scary and started being more uplifting. As an adult, Bianca uses her gift without fear, and she feels stronger than ever! She is also a mother now, and she can feel Mother Mary guiding her with her son. It is wonderful!

Notice how the scent of roses heralded the beginning of a vision for Bianca. In the following story, several people smelled roses simultaneously, lending further validation to this phenomenon:

Mother Mary has been an important part of **Rebecca Janelli**'s life since she was a child. She grew up in a Protestant home, with her mother changing religions as quickly as she changed friends, but Rebecca had always wished to be affiliated with the Catholic faith.

So, it was while she was in her mid-30s and experiencing one of the worst times of her life with an abusive husband that she converted to Catholicism. In fact, one Sunday Rebecca went to three different Catholic churches to find her new home. One priest she met on that day impressed her with his devotion and his modesty and humility, so she started going to church on a daily basis and found much solace there. She loved visiting Mother Mary's altar, and she prayed to her every day.

About a year and a half later, when Rebecca was at the lowest point in her marriage and was trying to care for her lovely young daughter, she started hearing Mother Mary, or at least, *feeling* her around her. The most amazing experience occurred on an afternoon when she was ill and at the end of her rope. Her own mother had been a stressed-out person who was abusive both mentally and physically while Rebecca was growing up. Mother Mary, she felt, was the mother she'd never really had.

Rebecca knelt down next to a rocking chair and placed her head on the seat, weak from illness, and asked Mother Mary for help. Almost immediately, she felt someone stroking her hair, and intense love and warmth surrounded her. She fell into a deep, peaceful sleep that lasted most of the afternoon. Upon waking up, Rebecca felt relaxed and uplifted, and although she tried to chalk it up to her imagination, she could not. That nap was the first good sleep she'd had in months!

A few weeks later, the priest's mother and several ladies from the parish came over to say the Rosary and have a Bible reading. Rebecca was a little late in joining them, as most of them had already arrived. But as soon as she entered the room, the ladies noted the heavy scent of roses, which Rebecca did not know until then could signify the Holy Mother's presence. She never wore rose perfume, or any that had roses as an ingredient, so the scent was pretty remarkable! However, Rebecca didn't question it. She simply relaxed and almost fell asleep while the Rosary was recited.

A few nights after that, a friend was taking her home in his new car, and they were driving through a dense fog on the dark interstate. The road was very slippery, and suddenly, they approached another car that was positioned sideways in the middle of both lanes. Rebecca's friend put on the brakes, but their car went out of control.

Rebecca screamed, "Help us, Mary!" Immediately, she felt the car slow down, and it almost felt like the bucket seats wrapped around them like soft cotton batting. Although they slid down a wet river embankment, they never went into the water, and the car wasn't damaged at all.

After the car came to a stop, Rebecca's friend asked her, "What was that you just screamed?"

She repeated what she had said, and her friend remarked, "I thought that's what you said. Who is Mary?"

Although he was a Baptist, and one who didn't believe that Mother Mary could have had any impact on their lives, Rebecca's friend admitted that there must have been Divine intervention involved.

Sometime subsequent to this event, Rebecca's health deteriorated into full-blown ovarian cancer! She was so ill that the doctors told her that she might have only two or three days to live. She had also been fired from her job and had no insurance. Things were about as bad as they could be, but Rebecca wasn't angry or bitter. She just hung on to her lovely crystal rosary beads, which she had been given the day she'd been confirmed into the Catholic Church.

One night while a priest was visiting her in the hospital, they recited the Rosary, and Rebecca started having nonstop visions of the Holy Mother's face. Again, she smelled roses, and saw images on the hospital wall of Calvary (the site of the Crucifixion), the Last Supper, and Jesus. At that moment, the string of rosary beads, which she had wrapped around the hospital bed, exploded and pieces flew everywhere.

The priest knelt on the floor along with one of her friends, and they saw the visions as well. Only two small crystal beads were found from her rosary; the rest were gone. A day later, the hospital chaplain came in with a new rosary . . . with special blessings from the Holy Virgin!

Rebecca had surgery about a day later, and remembered praying that if God wanted her, He could take her, but if she had a greater duty here, she would stay, no matter what. She woke up in excruciating pain, but she was alive; and when the doctors came in, they told her they had found *no cancer* anywhere in her abdomen.

Rebecca still communicates with Mother Mary and is so grateful for her intercession, which has allowed her to live healthy and happy from that time on!

❧

The rose fragrance helped Rebecca become calm so that healing could occur. Mother Mary makes her presence known, because she understands how comforted we are by the knowledge that she is there with us. The logical mind or the ego is skeptical about accepting signs from above, and may try to argue that the smell of roses is our imagination or that Mother Mary only visits people more "worthy." But the spiritual truth is that the Blessed Mother's power, presence, and love are unlimited and extend to all who call upon her.

The smell of roses is Mother Mary's calling card, in which she lets us know that she's watching over us and—as the next story so beautifully illustrates—our loved ones:

Back in September of 2003, **Kelly Casale**'s mother, Mary Lynn, passed away due to a tragic accident. A week to the day following the funeral, Kelly was home alone and decided to pray the Rosary.

After she completed her prayers, she felt at peace, and suddenly noticed a scent in the room, like freshly cut flowers. All the flowers left from the funeral had been disposed of three days prior, so she knew it wasn't that. So she started exploring where the scent was coming from, as the entire upstairs area of her home—the bathrooms, bedrooms, closets, and so on—smelled like roses!

A few years later, Kelly shared this story with a friend of hers, and the woman said to her, "When you smell roses, that is a sign Mother Mary is with you."

Well, that made sense to Kelly, since she had been praying the Rosary, after all. Looking back on it now, she definitely believes that Mother Mary was reassuring her that her family's own Mary (Mary Lynn) was safe and at peace.

❧

Mother Mary frequently sends rose fragrance to the bereaved, to signal that their loved ones are safely in heaven. In the following story, the scent of roses comforted a caring nurse after her patient's transition:

A woman whom I will call **Alexis** is a nurse who was once employed by a Catholic nursing home, a beautiful, spiritual place. She worked the 11 P.M. to 7 A.M. shift.

At that time she had a lovely patient, "Mrs. Smith," who was terminally ill with liver cancer. At that time, those who had liver cancer suffered a great deal of pain in spite of the medical profession's best efforts to keep them comfortable. Mrs. Smith never complained but endured many sleepless nights. Sometimes Alexis would sit in the chair beside Mrs. Smith's bed, saying the Rosary. During her rounds, she would ask Mrs. Smith if she wished to have medication prescribed for breakthrough pain, but she always refused.

Mrs. Smith's disease ran its course, and the time came when she was actively dying. She was in bed, in and out of consciousness. She was a widow and had no children, but she did have a nephew who was very, very devoted and who sat at her bedside as much as he could. (He was a middle-aged man with a family of his own who lived close by.)

One early morning, it was quite obvious that the end was near. Alexis entered the room to check on Mrs. Smith and her nephew, who asked if she thought his aunt would be passing away in the next couple of hours. She told him that she could not say with any accuracy. He was concerned, because he needed to get home in order to see that his children got on the school bus on time, but he didn't want to leave his aunt alone, either.

Alexis encouraged him to do what he needed to do—explaining that people often waited to cross over until someone was with them, but sometimes they didn't. Anyway, his need to help his children get ready for school compelled him to leave his aunt's bedside, with the promise that he would be back as soon as possible.

Alexis went on about her nursing rounds, and in the early morning was giving a report to the nurse who was coming on to relieve her. She went to Mrs. Smith's room just as she was preparing to leave. The nurse beckoned her from the doorway of the room. Alexis joined her there and discovered that indeed, Mrs. Smith had died. But the miraculous part of the story is that *the whole room was suffused with the scent of roses!*

There were no flowers, lotions, or perfumes of any kind in the room, nor had there ever been. There was no possible earthly explanation for the scent of roses in that room at that time, except for the fact that at her passing, she was met and accompanied by some heavenly beings who took her home, and who left behind the wonderful scent.

Alexis believes that Mrs. Smith's devotion to Mary and the saints, her frequent prayers, and her propensity to cast her pain and sorrows over to them enabled them to escort her home when her time had come.

How difficult it must be for health-care workers who bond with their patients and then witness those patients experiencing pain due to medical conditions. No wonder Mother Mary and the angels send them signs, such as the rose fragrance for Alexis. My prayer is that signs such as these help Alexis keep her caring heart open for her patients.

When we're frightened and need heaven the most, our fear may prevent us from feeling God's loving presence and hearing guidance from above. I believe that the Blessed

Mother sends the fragrance of roses as a sign that bypasses our fears, and brings us comfort in stressful situations.

I'm also struck by how many people have experiences with roses, without realizing their connection to Mother Mary. This, to me, shows that the rose scent goes way beyond imagination or wishful thinking, because it occurs when people have no idea of the fragrance's significance.

For many years, **Joshua Monzo** had felt the presence of Mother Mary in his life. When she comes around, she is accompanied by the incredible scent of roses, and a feeling of complete and unconditional love. His story involving Mother Mary is about his niece and his sister:

Joshua was sleeping one night when he got a call from his sister Chelsea. She was going into labor and was scared, so he called upon the angels and anyone who could help ease Chelsea's pain and bring her peace—especially since this was her first child.

Joshua told his sister not to worry, and that he would help by calling on Mother Mary and Archangel Gabriel. As he hung up the phone, he immediately asked that Mary and Gabriel surround his sister and his niece-to-be. He asked that they both remain healthy, and that his sister have a pain-free delivery. Right after requesting their aid, Joshua had the calming reassurance that all would be okay.

When he arrived at the hospital with his family to meet their newest family member, he was drawn to a statue of an angel kneeling down with its hands in prayer holding a Rosary. He knew that this was a sign from Mother Mary and Archangel Gabriel that everything was fine.

When he entered the room to see his sister and his niece, he was greeted by the scent of roses—a calling card of Mother Mary's to let him know that she was near. As he held his niece, Joshua looked into her eyes and felt the same absolute unconditional love that he always felt with Mother Mary. In that instant, he realized that the baby was one of the new Crystal Children here on Earth.

To this day, Joshua's niece, Taylor Rose, loves it when he calls on the angels and Mother Mary. She instantly becomes calmer and starts to giggle, as if they are putting on a show for her.

❧

Mother Mary helps all who call upon her, especially with situations involving beloved children. She aids everyone who is suffering, so that their lives may be more peaceful and harmonious. Such is the case in the following story, where Mother Mary brought happiness into the life of a woman who'd suffered in many ways:

Fifteen years ago, **Cathleen McCandless**'s mother (whose name, interestingly, was Mary) was diagnosed with stage IV terminal colon cancer. Cathleen was absolutely devastated. She and her mother were extremely close. They lived near each other, spent a great deal of time in each other's company, and traveled the world together. They were more like best friends or sisters than mother and daughter. Cathleen's mom was very kind, funny, and bright, and Cathleen's whole world fell apart when she got sick.

Cathleen's parents had divorced when she was young, and for the 22 years since they'd split up, her mom had been involved with a man I'll call Bert, who was a raging alcoholic. He was nasty and abusive to Mary, letting her down and disappointing her constantly. Cathleen and her sisters tried to get her to leave him, but she wouldn't. Instead, she endured his abuse year after year after year. It was difficult to see her mother, so loving and caring (and most likely codependent), putting up with this awful man.

Five days after her mom received her diagnosis, Cathleen was awakened in the middle of the night by the overpowering scent of roses in her bedroom. It was February, she had the windows closed, and she didn't even grow roses in her garden. But the smell was very strong (strong enough to wake her up), yet at the same time, quite delicate.

As Cathleen woke up, she saw a beautiful brown-haired woman standing at the foot of her bed, surrounded by a brilliant blue light. When Cathleen looked at her, she felt as if her heart was going to burst from the feeling of love she was filled with. In her entire life, Cathleen had never, ever experienced anything close to that feeling. The love was so intense that she felt as if her body couldn't contain it, and that she would almost die from the intensity of it.

The lady asked Cathleen telepathically, "What do you wish, dear one?"

Cathleen began to cry, saying that all she wanted was for her mother to get well. The lady shook her head and told her, "That is not God's will, and is something I cannot do. Is there anything else I can do for you?"

Cathleen blurted out without thinking, "If you can't make her well, then please give her someone to love for the remainder of her life."

The lady smiled and said, "That I will do. Is there anything else?"

Cathleen said no, and the lady then started to fade away, but as she did so, she said, "You know, dear one, it is all right to ask for something for yourself." (This was a lesson that Cathleen took a long time to learn.)

Although Cathleen had not been raised Catholic, she just *knew* that the beautiful lady was Mother Mary. At the time of the visitation, she had no idea that the Blessed Mother was associated with roses or the color blue, yet that is how she came to her. Cathleen didn't tell anyone about the visit. It was too personal (and a bit too strange) to share.

Four days afterward, Cathleen's mom was hosting a dinner party. Bert got drunk during the day, started a fight with Mary, and refused to come. Now Mary had no date for her own party, and she was very upset.

Anyway, that same day, Cathleen's mom, who lived in a condo complex, walked outside to get her mail. Standing at the mailboxes was Jack, one of her neighbors. She had seen him from time to time but didn't really know him. She introduced herself and told him that she was having a dinner party that night and asked if he would like to be her guest. He accepted the invitation, and from that very day, Cathleen's mom spent every day and night with Jack and never saw her old boyfriend again. She had spent 22 years with Bert, and that relationship ended the day she met Jack, who loved Mary totally and completely. Although she had been told she only had six months left, she went on to live for another year and a half, no doubt fueled by the love and care that Jack gave her.

Cathleen knew that when her mom met Jack, Mother Mary had kept her promise to her. The Blessed Mother had given her mother someone to love and be loved by until she died. Jack was holding her mom's right hand and Cathleen was holding her left the day she passed away; and believe it or not, Jack died on the exact same date one year later. Cathleen thinks it was due to a broken heart.

A few months after her mom started seeing Jack, they were all having dinner together, and Cathleen finally told everyone about the visit from Mother Mary and the promise she'd made. Everyone cried. Since that day, Cathleen has kept a picture of Mother Mary with her at all times. She can't begin to explain how much the Blessed Mother means to her.

On her birthday three years ago, Cathleen went to Fátima, Portugal. She made an offering in the basilica to thank Mother Mary for keeping her promise to her. She knows that the Blessed Mother is real because she has seen her. Cathleen has no doubt that she hears our prayers, feels our pain, and loves us more than any human being can imagine . . . just like a real mother.

Aren't these stories about roses so beautiful? How like Mother Mary to bring more beauty into our world in this way! I love this story about an actual rose that stayed perfectly preserved for over a month, with the help and blessings of Our Lady of the Roses:

Marcelle Lannaman was in between jobs, raising a family, and on a tight budget. Unable to buy her usual bouquet of roses for the Blessed Mother, she chose a magnificent single bloom: one that was cream colored and edged in scarlet. She placed it by a statue of Our Lady in her home.

"Blessed Mother, I wish I could buy you roses every week," Marcelle said.

Her solitary rose bloomed, and seemed to become fresher with each passing day. Two weeks later, it was still radiantly beautiful.

"Is that the same rose, Mum?" asked her son, Alexander, when he came home from school one day. They both gazed at it in awe and then took a picture of it.

Marcelle's "Mystical Rose" flourished for five weeks, never fading or wilting in any way.

On the first day of her new job, Marcelle came home to find that the petals had fallen at the feet of the Blessed Mother's statue. Whenever her faith in Divine Providence wavers, Marcelle affectionately remembers her eternal rose.

How blessed we are to have Mother Mary gracing us with signs of her love! Whether she appears to us in a dream or vision, or makes her presence known via a feeling, Divine intervention, or the fragrance of roses, it's comforting to be assured that she's hearing and answering our prayers.

CHAPTER TWELVE

SITES OF MARIAN VISIONS AND WORSHIP

Although you can commune with Mother Mary anywhere and everywhere, there are particular locations that are highly associated with her holy presence. These "Power Places" are the sites of profound visions, apparitions, sacred relics, and miraculous healings.

According to the Marian Library, in the past century the Catholic Church has received 386 reported cases of apparition sightings of Mother Mary, which have occurred upon every continent—to men, women, and children. An *apparition* refers to a person seeing, hearing, and having a solid, opaque experience of Mother Mary, with movement and speech, as opposed to the translucent visions within a person's mind's eye.

Of those cases, the church has investigated and substantiated eight as being definitely genuine. Many of the others are undecided, pending more investigation. And who knows how many unreported apparition experiences have occurred?

These eight officially sanctioned places where Mother Mary has appeared in the 20th century have become sites of pilgrimage for those seeking healing and enlightenment:

1. Fátima, Portugal

In 1917, on the 13th day of six consecutive months, three shepherd children saw and heard an apparition of Mother Mary. They described her as "brighter than the sun, shedding rays of light clearer and stronger than a crystal ball filled with the most sparkling water and pierced by the burning rays of the sun."

The apparition referred to herself as "the Lady of the Rosary," and she imparted three secrets to the children, which included prophetic information about the coming changes in Russia.

Today, Fátima is a sacred healing pilgrimage for millions.

2. Beauraing, Belgium

Between 1932 and 1933, five children had 33 apparition encounters with Mother Mary in which she repeatedly asked them to pray. She also requested that a chapel be built upon the site of her visitation so that people could visit it and receive healings.

3. Banneux, Belgium

In 1933, a teenage girl had several apparition visitations involving a woman identifying herself as "the Virgin of the Poor." Over a three-month period, Mother Mary asked the girl to drink from a healing spring. Today, this spring is visited by many people seeking its healing water.

4. Akita, Japan

A nun named Sister Agnes, who'd suffered from health conditions, had an apparition encounter with Mother Mary in 1973. She also had stigmata (spontaneous wounds similar to those of Christ during the Crucifixion). Notably, a Virgin Mary statue at Akita wept unexplainable tears more than 100 times, and these tears were visible on television.

5. Syracuse, Italy

A newlywed couple named Antonina and Angelo Iannuso received a plaster wall plaque of the Virgin Mary as a wedding gift in 1953. When Antonina conceived a child, she suffered from toxemia, which led to convulsions and temporary blindness. She recovered, and noticed that her Virgin Mary statue was shedding tears. Many people saw, and even tasted, these tears. An investigation into the tears concluded that this was a genuine case of a weeping Virgin Mary statue. Nearly 300 people have reported receiving miraculous healings from the statue, including Antonina, who recovered from toxemia and gave birth to a healthy baby on Christmas Day.

6. Zeitoun, Egypt

In 1968, a group of people saw a woman standing atop a Catholic church and feared she was trying to commit suicide. Soon, however, they realized they were seeing Mother Mary. She continued to appear as an apparition two to three times a week until 1971. It's estimated that between 250,000 and one million people witnessed the apparition in person.

7. Manila, Philippines

In 1948, a Carmelite nun named Teresita Catillo experienced 19 apparition visitations from Mother Mary. Rose petals began spontaneously appearing where the

Blessed Mother had appeared, and people reported healings arising from these petals.

8. Betania, Venezuela

In 1974, a woman named Maria Esperanza was guided to an agricultural property through detailed instructions she'd received from Mother Mary during visions. In 1976, Maria had an apparition experience with Mother Mary at the location she'd been guided to. In 1984, 150 people saw Mother Mary together, and this group included dignitaries and medical and legal professionals.

The Mother Mary apparitions at most of these sites have delivered similar messages: pray the Rosary and do penances. In many visitations, Mary emphasized that only she or Jesus could save people from impending catastrophe. Indeed, many of the locations of Mother Mary apparitions were subject to war and natural disaster, so her messages were prophetic.

Other Notable Marian Shrines

The number of people who have reported miraculous healings and apparition encounters with Mother Mary has increased in recent years. They are too numerous to recount in this book. However, here are some other notable sites of Mother Mary experiences:

Lourdes, France

While young Bernadette Soubirous was out gathering firewood in 1858, she encountered an apparition of Mother

Mary. Over the course of six months, Bernadette received 18 visits, during which Mother Mary instructed her to dig in the ground. A spring of water began to appear. Bernadette and her parents were threatened with legal and psychiatric punishment if the girl didn't stop talking about her encounters with Mother Mary. The persecution stopped when people who bathed in the Lourdes springwater underwent miraculous healing. Today, millions of people pilgrimage to Lourdes, and more than 60 miraculous healings have been documented.

Medjugorje, Yugoslavia

Six young people simultaneously experienced an apparition of Mother Mary over several visits, in which she gave prophetic warnings to pray and fast to avoid world catastrophes. The Blessed Mother imparted secrets to the youths, who were totally oblivious to outside sounds and lights when they were experiencing an apparition. Millions of people have traveled to this sacred site for prayer and healing.

Guadalupe, Mexico

As an Aztec named Juan Diego was walking, a beautiful woman glowing with light appeared to him. She identified herself as Mother Mary and requested that a church be built on the spot where they stood so that she could help people in the vicinity. Juan relayed this request to the local archbishop, who asked Juan to get proof from the woman that she was in fact the Virgin Mary.

When Juan asked Mother Mary for assistance with this proof, she instructed him to gather roses at a specific location, even though it was the height of winter. Juan found many roses, which he gathered in his cloak, or *tilma*. When Juan opened his tilma before the archbishop, the roses fell to the ground, and inside was the image of Our Lady of Guadalupe. The tilma is preserved at the Basilica of Guadalupe in Mexico City, where millions of pilgrims visit.

Stories from Those Who Have Visited Marian Sites

Here are some stories from people who have had profound experiences at Mother Mary shrines:

Lourdes: **Kerri**, from Dublin, Ireland, is profoundly deaf. Years ago, when she was in her final year of high school, she was having a hard time. Certain people had been making her miserable for a long time, and all this was finally coming to a head.

It just so happened that Kerri's mother was taking a trip to Lourdes that week, but she was so worried about Kerri that she almost decided not to go. However, Kerri insisted that her mom take the trip because she knew what a special place Lourdes was. Kerri told her mother she'd be just fine at home with her dad.

Her mom thought it would be good for Kerri to get away, too, so she phoned the travel agency to see if there were any available spaces on the tour she was going on. Unfortunately, it was booked solid.

The night before her mom was due to leave, Kerri had a very realistic dream, where she was seeing her mother off at the Dublin airport. Our Lady was standing at the bottom of the steps of the airplane on the tarmac, absolutely glowing, and she had a beautiful human face that was beaming with joy. Mother Mary was waving at Kerri, pointing to the steps, indicating that she should board the plane and go to

Lourdes. It was such a vivid dream, and when Kerri woke up, she had such a warm feeling!

The next morning, she told her mom about the dream, and they were both very intrigued. Later in the day, the phone rang and it was the travel agency. It turned out that a place on the tour had opened up for Kerri overnight! Apparently a man had taken ill suddenly and was unable to make the trip, so they asked Kerri's mom if her daughter was still interested in going. Of course she said yes.

Kerri almost couldn't believe her luck, but when she thought about her lovely dream from the night before, she was certain that Mother Mary wanted her to go to Lourdes and get the solace she needed to cope with her final year at school.

The trip did just that, and Kerri and her mother will be forever grateful to the Blessed Mother!

Fátima: In August 2008, **Trude** went on a vacation with her sister to Lisbon, Portugal. At the time, she was working very hard, pursuing a legal career, and she was also an elected local politician. For a long time, she had felt a draining energy around her workplace and her political life, but she feared that if she let go of these ambitions, she would not be as successful as she wanted to be.

Trude's personal life was rather chaotic, too, as she had met Rolf, a wonderful man, in 2003 when he was looking for a legal advisor. They'd felt an instant attraction, and loved and respected one another, but circumstances made it impossible for them to be together. At least, so it seemed at the time.

For a while, Trude had been reading my books, and she related to the fact that we were both academics with university degrees; yet I was able to use my spiritual gifts, and she hadn't been able to yet. In the past, I had written about the different power places in the world, and by coincidence, Trude realized that just a bit north of Lisbon was Fátima, a sacred place with Mother Mary's energy and presence.

Upon arrival in Fátima, Trude instantly felt a calming energy—like that of a mother caring for her children. She went to the sacred place in front of the church built in Mary's honor and put some holy water on her forehead and neck, and then prayed: "Mother Mary, can you please heal the parts of my life that aren't working. Can you please help me be completely happy."

Trude was so stressed at the time because she was used to a huge workload with legal cases, so she was unable to just stand still and focus. She started taking pictures when she felt Mother Mary's presence, and her camera shut down twice even though the batteries were fully charged. The second time it happened, Trude was sure it was because Mary was there with her, listening to her. The message seemed to be: *I am here with you, so you don't need to take any more pictures, as you will remember my presence.*

On the way back to Lisbon, Trude started to get sick, and her condition became worse over the next few hours. It turned out that she had a life-threatening inflammation of the brain and had to be hospitalized. Her face was partly paralyzed, and she had problems speaking, hearing, using her hands, and walking. She remembers thinking that she didn't know what physical pain was until she experienced this. She prayed that the pain would go away, saying that she couldn't take it anymore. Trude got the instant feeling that she should try to lie completely still, so she did.

It was difficult for her to discern one day from the next, but she does remember being so sick that she knew she had choice: she could leave and go to the Other Side, or she could stay here and finish her life. She remembers going back and forth between the two options, and how her pain lessened as she went toward the Other Side, but then she stopped herself, thinking that there were so many dreams she had for *this* life, and she just couldn't leave. Then the pain would become more intense as she leaned toward life and fought to open her eyes and focus. She was very sick for nine days and knew that she could die at any time, but she held on to the feeling of Mother Mary's presence to help her get through the ordeal.

During Trude's stay in the hospital, her sister told her that Rolf had called, and she'd told him that Trude was in a hospital in Lisbon and that her condition was serious. Rolf later told her he knew that there was a chance she could die even though her sister didn't tell him that, and he was naturally very worried. He started sending Trude text messages, where he stated how much he loved her and that he wanted to be with her.

When Trude got better, she and Rolf got back together, and he proposed to her in July 2009. They got married in Tahiti and spent a romantic honeymoon in the islands of Bora Bora and Moorea.

This experience completely changed Trude's life, as well as Rolf's. They feel that due to the miracle of Mother Mary's love, Trude survived her ordeal and was able to have the wonderful relationship she'd always dreamed of.

Trude and Rolf now share an office and have created the perfect work space. The greatest miracle they experienced through Mother Mary is that of unconditional love. They believe that Mary brought them together and made them realize their twin-flame connection. She taught them that only love is real!

Lourdes Grotto, Texas: **Linda Clements** had just moved to San Antonio, Texas, and had gotten involved with a prayer group. She and the group leader had become good friends, and they prayed often to Mother Mary—powerful, healing prayers. Her friend really educated her about who Mary was, and the role she played in her own life.

Through her friend, Linda found out about a wonderful place called the Oblate School of Theology, a seminary where Mary's presence was very powerful. One day Linda visited the grounds, where there is a replica of the Lourdes Grotto, which had been dedicated on Linda's birthday in 1942. There was also a tiny chapel, with a wonderful mosaic of Our Lady of Guadalupe on top of it. Linda admired the simple mosaic, and saw how lovingly it had been created.

As Linda turned to go, she heard a very clear voice ask, "Don't you have even a few moments for her?"

Linda turned around and exclaimed, "Yes, ma'am!" She sat for a while, listening, telling Our Lady that she would be happy to hear what she had to say.

Mother Mary said, "Just ask."

So Linda *would* ask, many times over the years. She would kneel in prayer or tears or joy, and she would leave gifts of flowers or money when she could. Downstairs, people could light candles in the grotto, and she did that at times, too.

One day Linda tried to take some pictures of Mary and the grotto. When she got the prints back, there was a nebulous white cloud in the middle. She was rather disappointed, but her friend who led the prayer group and others said it was a sign that Mother Mary would always be with her. She never again questioned that presence or the information she received, although sometimes it was most unexpected.

Linda tried to follow the guidance she was given, and was often joyously surprised by the results.

Linda moved to a different city, and whenever she returns to San Antonio, she spends time at the seminary, always feeling so much peace there.

Visiting a Marian shrine such as Lourdes or Fátima can be life changing and healing. For me, these locations associated with Mother Mary help me feel even closer to her. Prayers I've said at some of them have been instantly answered in powerful and unexpected ways. I believe that the power of millions of people praying in the same location creates a clear portal to heaven.

The fact is, though, that Mother Mary is available to everyone everywhere simultaneously. You can call upon her from any location and in any way. In the Appendix that follows, I've listed a few traditional and modern prayers for your reference. However, please know that Mother Mary responds to your heartfelt appeals, no matter how they are worded or where they're said.

Mother Mary is our universal maternal guide who loves all of us unconditionally and purely. She can fill and heal any gaps in your heart where you have "mother" wounds or a need for nurturing.

I believe that Mother Mary wants to help us *all* be at peace . . . because she cares about you, me, and every one of us on this planet. I'm convinced that Mother Mary is enacting God's plan of peace on Earth by helping each of us live our lives more peacefully together. By working with Mother Mary, you tap into the Divine plan of peace and become part of the solution.

APPENDIX

Biblical References to Mother Mary

These are the references from the Gospels (King James Version) in which Mary is specifically named:

And Jacob begat Joseph the husband of Mary, of whom was born Jesus, who is called Christ.

(Matthew 1:16)

Now the birth of Jesus Christ was on this wise: When as his mother Mary was espoused to Joseph, before they came together, she was found with child of the Holy Ghost.

Then Joseph her husband, being a just man, and not willing to make her a public example, was minded to put her away privily.

But while he thought on these things, behold, the angel of the Lord appeared unto him in a dream, saying, Joseph, thou son of David, fear not to take unto thee Mary thy wife: for that which is conceived in her is of the Holy Ghost.

And she shall bring forth a son, and thou shalt call his
name Jesus: for he shall save his people from their sins.

Now all this was done, that it might be fulfilled which
was spoken of the Lord by the prophet, saying,

Behold, a virgin shall be with child, and shall bring
forth a son, and they shall call his name Emmanuel,
which being interpreted is, God with us.

Then Joseph being raised from sleep did as the angel of
the Lord had bidden him, and took unto him his wife:

And knew her not till she had brought forth her
firstborn son: and he called his name Jesus.

(Matthew 1:18–25)

And when they were come into the house, they saw
the young child with Mary his mother, and fell down,
and worshipped him: and when they had opened their
treasures, they presented unto him gifts; gold,
and frankincense and myrrh.

(Matthew 2:11)

And when they were come into the house, they saw
the young child with Mary his mother, and fell down,

Is not this the carpenter's son? Is not his mother
called Mary?

(Matthew 13:55)

And in the sixth month the angel Gabriel was sent
from God unto a city of Galilee, named Nazareth,

To a virgin espoused to a man whose name was Joseph,
of the house of David; and the virgin's name was Mary.

And the angel came in unto her, and said, Hail, thou
that art highly favoured, the Lord is with thee:
blessed art thou among women.

And when she saw him, she was troubled at his saying,
and cast in her mind what manner of salutation this
should be.

And the angel said unto her, Fear not, Mary:
for thou hast found favour with God.

And, behold, thou shalt conceive in thy womb, and
bring forth a son, and shalt call his name JESUS.

He shall be great, and shall be called the Son of the
Highest: and the Lord God shall give unto him
the throne of his father David:

And he shall reign over the house of Jacob for ever;
and of his kingdom there shall be no end.

Then said Mary unto the angel, How shall this be,
seeing I know not a man?

And the angel answered and said unto her, The Holy
Ghost shall come upon thee, and the power of the
Highest shall overshadow thee: therefore also that
holy thing which shall be born of thee shall be
called the Son of God.

And, behold, thy cousin Elisabeth, she hath also
conceived a son in her old age: and this is the
sixth month with her, who was called barren.

For with God nothing shall be impossible.

And Mary said, Behold the handmaid of the Lord;
be it unto me according to thy word. And the
angel departed from her.

And Mary arose in those days, and went into
the hill country with haste, into a city of Juda;

And entered into the house of Zacharias,
and saluted Elisabeth.

And it came to pass, that, when Elisabeth heard the
salutation of Mary, the babe leaped in her womb;
and Elisabeth was filled with the Holy Ghost:

And she spake out with a loud voice, and said, Blessed
art thou among women, and blessed is the fruit of
thy womb.

And whence is this to me, that the mother of my
Lord should come to me?

For, lo, as soon as the voice of thy salutation sounded
in mine ears, the babe leaped in my womb for joy.

And blessed is she that believed: for there shall be a
performance of those things which were told her
from the Lord.

And Mary said, My soul doth magnify the Lord,

And my spirit hath rejoiced in God my Saviour.

For he hath regarded the low estate of his handmaiden:
for, behold, from henceforth all generations shall
call me blessed.

For he that is mighty hath done to me great things;
and holy is his name.

And his mercy is on them that fear him from
generation to generation.

He hath shewed strength with his arm; he hath
scattered the proud in the imagination of their hearts.

He hath put down the mighty from their seats,
and exalted them of low degree.

He hath filled the hungry with good things; and the
rich he hath sent empty away.

He hath helped his servant Israel, in remembrance of his
mercy;

As he spake to our fathers, to Abraham, and to his
seed for ever.

And Mary abode with her about three months, and
returned to her own house.

(Luke 1:26–56)

❧

And it came to pass in those days, that there went out a
decree from Caesar Augustus that all the world should
be taxed.

(And this taxing was first made when Cyrenius
was governor of Syria.)

And all went to be taxed, every one into his own city.

And Joseph also went up from Galilee, out of the city of
Nazareth, into Judaea, unto the city of David, which
is called Bethlehem; (because he was of the house and
lineage of David:)

To be taxed with Mary his espoused wife, being great
with child.

And so it was, that, while they were there, the days
were accomplished that she should be delivered.

And she brought forth her firstborn son, and wrapped
him in swaddling clothes, and laid him in a manger;
because there was no room for them in the inn.

(**Luke 2:1–7**)

Is not this the carpenter, the son of Mary, the brother
of James, and Joses, and of Juda, and Simon?

(**Mark 6:3**)

All these with one accord were devoting themselves to
prayer, together with the women and Mary the mother
of Jesus, and his brothers.

(**Acts 1:14**)

Modern Prayers to Mother Mary

In this section, you'll find prayers to Mother Mary that are nontraditional and take an affirmative approach in their wording. You are invited to personalize them and create your own prayers as well. Mother Mary responds to the intention behind the prayer, not the words themselves.

Prayer for Another Person's Health

Dear Mother Mary,

I ask for your intervention with respect to *[name of person]*'s health and wellness. Please take *[name]* into your loving arms and nurture him/her back to health, according to God's will and plan for him/her. Please keep *[name]* safe, protected, and comfortable. Please clearly guide me as to how I can best support *[name]* on his/her journey of health. Amen.

Prayer for Child Conception

Dear Blessed Mother Mary,

I have so much love to give and deeply desire to share it with my child. Thank for gracing me with your support in conceiving a child. I ask that you clearly guide me in taking action steps that will help me conceive, carry, and give birth to a healthy son or daughter. Thank you and amen.

ॐ

Prayer for Emotional Healing

Dearest Mother Mary,

Thank you for healing my heart. Thank you for holding me in your loving arms and surrounding me with your purifying nurturing so that I feel safe, loved, and happy. I ask that you help me let go of the past, and move forward with grace and ease. Amen.

ॐ

Prayer for Global Peace

Dear Mother Mary,

I care so deeply for this world and all of its inhabitants, and I know that you are watching over all of us on our beautiful planet. Thank you for helping me see and feel your presence, so that I may feel safe about our future. Please clearly guide me as to how I can be of service to God's will for peace upon Earth. Amen.

Prayer for Inner Peace

Dear Beloved Mother,

I desire to have the peace of God in my heart, body, and mind, and ask for your Divine intercession in bringing me inner peace. I now willingly give to you and God all of my burdens and sorrows, knowing that you will gladly take them to heaven, where there are ingenious solutions to all seeming problems. Thank you for shining Divine light into me, so that my faith and happiness are restored. Amen.

Prayer for a Physical Healing

Dear Mother Mary,

I know that God created my body in His image and likeness, and therefore I am healthy in spiritual truth. I pray for your purifying love to help heal my experience of my body, so that I may enjoy health and vitality. Please put your loving arms around me and shine your healing light into every cell of my physical being, restoring and balancing me back to Divine health. Amen.

Prayer for Protection

Dear Blessed Mother,

Thank you for watching over me, my loved ones, my vehicle, and my home and for protecting us in all ways. I ask that you shield us in a blanket of love so that we are protected physically, emotionally, spiritually, energetically, intellectually, and financially. Thank you and amen.

Prayer for a Relationship (Existing)

Dear Mother Mary,

I have been feeling *[describe your emotions]* about my relationship with *[name of person]*. I ask for your Divine assistance in restoring peace, love, honesty, respect, and understanding to our relationship. Please help us to be in harmonious partnership with one another and focused upon a unified goal of mutual happiness. Thank you and amen.

Prayer for a Relationship (New)

Dear Beloved Mother Mary,

My heart yearns for great love within a romantic partnership. Please help me prepare for and meet a romantic partner with whom I can commit to a long-term healthy and happy love relationship. Thank you for helping my heart to be healed, open, and ready for true love. Amen.

Prayer for Supply

Dear Blessed Mother,

Thank you for watching over my loved ones and me, ensuring that our needs for a safe, comfortable home; clean drinking water; adequate clothing; healthful food; school supplies; and other basics are met. Please help us to experience a steady flow of supply in exchange for our honest work. Thank you for being the way-shower of how I may navigate within the world of careers and finances, while staying true to myself, my soul, and God. Amen.

Traditional Catholic Mother Mary Prayers, Novena, and Liturgies

Here are some prayers from the Catholic faith that are traditional ways of appealing to Mother Mary for intercession. These prayers use words that may trigger some people, such as references to sinners. Others may find comfort in the traditional nature of these prayers, so they are included for reference and for those who prefer a classic approach to prayer.

Hail Mary

Hail Mary,
Full of Grace,
The Lord is with thee.
Blessed art thou among women,
and blessed is the fruit
of thy womb, Jesus.
Holy Mary,
Mother of God,
pray for us sinners now,
and at the hour of death.
Amen.

Children's Prayer to Mary

Dear Mother of Jesus,
look down upon me
As I say my prayers slowly
at my mother's knee.

I love thee, O Lady,
and please willest thou bring
All little children
To Jesus our King.

Novena (Nine-Day) Prayer
of the Immaculate Conception

(First, recite the Prayer to the Immaculate Conception below. Then recite the appropriate prayer of each of the nine days.)

Oh God, who by the Immaculate Conception of the Blessed Virgin Mary, did prepare a worthy dwelling place for Your Son, we beseech You that, as by the foreseen death of this, Your Son, You did preserve Her from all stain, so too You would permit us, purified through Her intercession, to come unto You. Through the same Lord Jesus Christ, Your Son, who lives and reigns with You in the unity of the Holy Spirit, God, world without end. Amen.

Day One

O most Holy Virgin, who was pleasing to the Lord and became His mother, immaculate in body and spirit, in faith and in love, look kindly on me as I implore your powerful intercession. Oh most Holy Mother, who by your blessed Immaculate Conception, from the first moment of your conception did crush the head of the enemy, receive our prayers as we implore you to present at the throne of God the favor we now request . . .

(State your intention here . . .)

Oh Mary of the Immaculate Conception, Mother of Christ, you had influence with your Divine Son while upon this earth; you have the same influence now in heaven. Pray for us and obtain for us from him the granting of my petition if it be the Divine Will. Amen.

Day Two

Oh Mary, ever blessed Virgin, Mother of God, Queen of angels and of saints, we salute you with the most profound veneration and filial devotion as we contemplate your holy Immaculate Conception, We thank you for your maternal protection and for the many blessings that we have received through your wondrous mercy and most powerful intercession. In all our necessities we have recourse to you with unbounded confidence. Oh Mother of Mercy, we beseech you now to hear our prayer and to obtain for us of your Divine Son the favor that we so earnestly request in this novena . . .

(State your intention here . . .)

Oh Mary of the Immaculate Conception, Mother of Christ, you had influence with your Divine Son while upon this earth; you have the same influence now in heaven. Pray for us and obtain for us from him the granting of my petition if it be the Divine Will. Amen.

Day Three

O Blessed Virgin Mary, glory of the Christian people, joy of the universal Church and Mother of Our Lord, speak for us to the Heart of Jesus, who is your Son and our brother. Oh Mary, who by your holy Immaculate Conception did enter the world free from stain, in your mercy obtain for us from Jesus the special favor which we now so earnestly seek . . .

(State your intention here . . .)

Oh Mary of the Immaculate Conception, Mother of Christ, you had influence with your Divine Son while upon this earth; you have the same influence now in heaven. Pray for us and obtain for us from him the granting of my petition if it be the Divine Will. Amen.

Day Four

O Mary, Mother of God, endowed in your glorious Immaculate Conception with the fullness of grace; unique among women in that you are both mother and virgin; Mother of Christ and Virgin of Christ, we ask you to look down with a tender heart from your throne and listen to our prayers as we earnestly ask that you obtain for us the favor for which we now plead . . .

(State your intention here . . .)

Oh Mary of the Immaculate Conception, Mother of Christ, you had influence with your Divine Son while upon this earth; you have the same influence now in heaven. Pray for us and obtain for us from him the granting of my petition if it be the Divine Will. Amen.

Day Five

Oh Lord, who, by the Immaculate Conception of the Virgin Mary, did prepare a fitting dwelling for your Son, we beseech you that as by the foreseen death of your Son, you did preserve her from all stain of sin, grant that through her intercession, we may be favored with the granting of the grace that we seek for at this time . . .

(State your intention here . . .)

Oh Mary of the Immaculate Conception, Mother of Christ, you had influence with your Divine Son while upon this earth; you have the same influence now in heaven. Pray for us and obtain for us from him the granting of my petition if it be the Divine Will. Amen.

Day Six

Glorious and immortal Queen of Heaven, we profess our firm belief in your Immaculate Conception preordained for you in the merits of your Divine Son. We rejoice with you in your Immaculate Conception. To the one ever-reigning God, Father, Son, and Holy Spirit, three in Person, one in nature, we offer thanks for your blessed Immaculate Conception. Oh Mother of the Word made Flesh, listen to our petition as we ask this special grace during this novena . . .

(State your intention here . . .)

Oh Mary of the Immaculate Conception, Mother of Christ, you had influence with your Divine Son while upon this earth; you have the same influence now in heaven. Pray for us and obtain for us from him the granting of my petition if it be the Divine Will. Amen.

Day Seven

Oh Immaculate Virgin, Mother of God, and my mother, from the sublime heights of your dignity turn your merciful eyes upon me while I, full of confidence in your bounty and keeping in mind your Immaculate conception and fully conscious of your power, beg of you to come to our aid and ask your Divine Son to grant the favor we earnestly seek in this novena . . . if it be beneficial for our immortal souls and the souls for whom we pray.

(State your intention here . . .)

Oh Mary of the Immaculate Conception, Mother of Christ, you had influence with your Divine Son while upon this earth; you have the same influence now in heaven. Pray for us and obtain for us from him the granting of my petition if it be the Divine Will. Amen.

Day Eight

Oh Most gracious Virgin Mary, beloved Mother of Jesus Christ, our Redeemer, intercede with him for us that we be granted the favor which we petition for so earnestly in this novena . . . Oh Mother of the Word Incarnate, we feel animated with confidence that your prayers in our behalf will be graciously heard before the throne of God. Oh Glorious Mother of God, in memory of your joyous Immaculate Conception, hear our prayers and obtain for us our petitions . . .

(State your intention here . . .)

Oh Mary of the Immaculate Conception, Mother of Christ, you had influence with your Divine Son while upon this earth; you have the same influence now in heaven. Pray for us and obtain for us from him the granting of my petition if it be the Divine Will. Amen.

Day Nine

Oh Mother of the King of the Universe, most perfect member of the human race, "our tainted nature's solitary boast," we turn to you as mother, advocate, and mediatrix. Oh Holy Mary, assist us in our present necessity. By your Immaculate Conception, Oh Mary conceived without sin, we humbly beseech you from the bottom of our heart to intercede for us with your Divine Son and ask that we be granted the favor for which we now plead . . .

(State your intention here . . .)

Oh Mary of the Immaculate Conception, Mother of Christ, you had influence with your Divine Son while upon this earth; you have the same influence now in heaven. Pray for us and obtain for us from him the granting of my petition if it be the Divine Will. Amen.

Litany of the Blessed Virgin

Lord, have mercy on us
Christ, have mercy on us
Lord, have mercy on us
Christ, hear us
Christ, graciously hear us

God the Father of heaven, have mercy on us, God the Son, Redeemer of the World, have mercy on us, God the Holy Spirit . . .

Holy Trinity, one God . . .
Holy Mary, pray for us
Holy Mother of God, pray for us
Holy Virgin of virgins . . .
Mother of Christ . . .
Mother of Divine Grace . . .
Mother most pure . . .
Mother most chaste . . .
Mother inviolate . . .

Mother undefiled . . .
Mother most amiable . . .
Mother most admirable . . .
Mother of good counsel . . .
Mother of our Creator . . .
Mother of our Savior . . .
Virgin most prudent . . .
Virgin most venerable . . .
Virgin most renowned . . .
Virgin most powerful . . .
Virgin most merciful . . .
Virgin most faithful . . .
Mirror of justice . . .
Seat of wisdom . . .
Cause of our joy . . .
Spiritual vessel . . .
Vessel of honor . . .
Singular vessel of devotion . . .
Mystical rose . . .
Tower of David . . .
Tower of ivory . . .
House of gold . . .
Ark of the covenant . . .
Gate of heaven . . .
Morning star . . .
Health of the sick . . .
Refuge of sinners . . .
Comforter of the afflicted . . .
Help of Christians . . .
Queen of Angels . . .
Queen of Patriarchs . . .
Queen of Prophets . . .
Queen of Apostles . . .

Queen of Martyrs . . .
Queen of Confessors . . .
Queen of Virgins . . .
Queen of all Saints . . .
Queen conceived without original sin . . .
Queen assumed into heaven . . .
Queen of the most holy Rosary . . .
Queen of Peace . . .

Lamb of God, who takes away the sins of the world, spare us, O Lord, Lamb of God, who takes away the sins of the world, graciously hear us, O Lord, Lamb of God, who takes away the sins of the world, have mercy on us.

Grant we beseech Thee, O Lord God, that we, Thy servants, may enjoy perpetual health of mind and body: and, by the glorious intercession of the blessed Mary, ever Virgin, be delivered from present sorrow and enjoy eternal gladness.

Through Christ, our Lord.
Amen.

Consecration to Mary Prayer

Oh Mary, Virgin most powerful and Mother of mercy, Queen of Heaven and Refuge of sinners, we consecrate ourselves to thine Immaculate Heart.

We consecrate to thee our very being and our whole life; all that we have, all that we love, all that we are. To thee we give our bodies, our hearts and our souls; to thee we give our homes, our families, our country.

We desire that all that is in us and around us may belong to thee, and may share in the benefits of thy motherly benediction. And that this act of consecration may be truly efficacious and lasting, we renew this day at thy feet the promises of our Baptism and our first Holy Communion.

We pledge ourselves to profess courageously and at all times the truths of our holy Faith, and to live as befits Catholics who are duly submissive to all the directions of the Pope and the Bishops in communion with him.

We pledge ourselves to keep the commandments of God and His Church, in particular to keep holy the Lord's Day.

We likewise pledge ourselves to make the consoling practices of the Christian religion, and above all, Holy Communion, an integral part of our lives, in so far as we shall be able so to do.

Finally, we promise thee, O glorious Mother of God and loving Mother of men, to devote ourselves whole-heartedly to the service of thy blessed cult, in order to hasten and assure, through the sovereignty of thine Immaculate Heart, the coming of the kingdom of the Sacred Heart of thine adorable Son, in our own hearts and in those of all men, in our country and in all the world, as in heaven, so on earth. Amen.

Memorare Prayer

Remember, O most gracious Virgin Mary, that never was it known that anyone who fled to thy protection, implored thy help, or sought thine intercession was left unaided.

Inspired by this confidence, I fly unto thee, O Virgin of virgins, my mother; to thee do I come, before thee I stand, sinful and sorrowful. O Mother of the Word Incarnate, despise not my petitions, but in thy mercy hear and answer me. Amen.

Regina Coeli Prayer

Queen of Heaven, rejoice, alleluia.
For He whom you did merit to bear, alleluia.

Has risen, as he said, alleluia.
Pray for us to God, alleluia.

Rejoice and be glad, O Virgin Mary, alleluia.
For the Lord has truly risen, alleluia.

Let us pray. O God, who gave joy to the world through the resurrection of Thy Son, our Lord Jesus Christ, grant we beseech Thee, that through the intercession of the Virgin Mary, His Mother, we may obtain the joys of everlasting life. Through the same Christ our Lord. Amen.

Prayer to Our Lady of Guadalupe

Our Lady of Guadalupe,
Mystical Rose,
make intercession for holy Church,
protect the sovereign Pontiff,
help all those who invoke you in their necessities,
and since you are the ever Virgin Mary
and Mother of the true God,
obtain for us from your most holy Son
the grace of keeping our faith,
of sweet hope in the midst of the bitterness of life
of burning charity, and the precious gift
of final perseverance.
Amen.

Angelus Prayer

The Angel of the Lord declared to Mary:
And she conceived of the Holy Spirit. Hail Mary, full
of grace, the Lord is with thee; blessed art thou among
women and blessed is the fruit of thy womb, Jesus. Holy
Mary, Mother of God, pray for us sinners, now and at the
hour of our death. Amen. Behold the handmaid of the
Lord: Be it done unto me according to Thy word.
Hail Mary . . . And the Word was made Flesh: And dwelt
among us. Hail Mary . . .
Pray for us, O Holy Mother of God, that we may be made
worthy of the promises of Christ.

Let us pray: Pour forth, we beseech Thee, O Lord, Thy grace into our hearts; that we, to whom the incarnation of Christ, Thy Son, was made known by the message of an angel, may by His Passion and Cross be brought to the glory of His Resurrection, through the same Christ Our Lord. Amen.

Prayer for Health

Virgin, most holy, Mother of the Word Incarnate, Treasurer of graces, and Refuge of sinners, I fly top your motherly affection with lively faith, and I beg of you the grace ever to do the will of God.

Into your most holy hands I commit the keeping of my heart, asking you for health of soul and body, in the certain hope that you, my most loving Mother, will hear my prayer.

Into the bosom of your tender mercy, this day, every day of my life, and at the hour of my death, I commend my soul and body.

To you I entrust all my hopes and consolations, all my trials and miseries, my life and the end of my life, that all my actions may be ordered and disposed according to your will and that of your Divine Son. Amen.

Mother of Perpetual Help Prayer

Oh Mother of Perpetual Help, grant that I may ever invoke
your powerful name, the protection of the living and
the salvation of the dying. Purest Mary, let your name
henceforth be ever on my lips. Delay not, Blessed Lady, to
rescue me whenever I call on you. In my temptations, in
my needs, I will never cease to call on you, ever repeating
your sacred name, Mary, Mary. What a consolation, what
sweetness, what confidence fills my soul when I utter your
sacred name or even only think of you! I thank the Lord
for having given you so sweet, so powerful, so lovely a
name. But I will not be content with merely uttering your
name. Let my love for your prompt me ever to hail you
Mother of Perpetual Help.

Mother of Perpetual Help, pray for me and grant me the
favor I confidently ask of you . . .

(Mention your petition . . .)

Prayer to Our Lady of Lourdes

Oh ever-Immaculate Virgin, Mother of Mercy,
health of the sick, refuge of sinners,
comforter of the afflicted,
you know my wants, my troubles, my sufferings;
look with mercy on me.

By appearing in the Grotto of Lourdes,
you were pleased to make it a privileged sanctuary,
whence you dispense your favors;

and already many sufferers have obtained
the cure of their infirmities, both spiritual and corporal.

I come, therefore, with complete confidence
to implore your maternal intercession.

Obtain, O loving Mother, the grant of my requests.
Through gratitude for your favors,
I will endeavor to imitate your virtues,
that I may one day share your glory. Amen.

Salve Regina Prayer

Hail, holy Queen, Mother of mercy,
hail, our life, our sweetness, and our hope.
To you we cry, the children of Eve;
to you we send up our sighs,
mourning and weeping in this land of exile.
Turn, then, most gracious advocate,
your eyes of mercy toward us;
lead us home at last
and show us the blessed fruit of your womb, Jesus:
O clement, O loving, O sweet virgin Mary.
Amen.

Blessed Mother Prayer

May the Blessed Mother come
into your life today with
a special blessing for you.
May you always be grateful for
the Blessed Mother.
Without her we would not have
Jesus. Our Savior.

Prayer to the Queen of Angels

Immaculate Virgin, Mother of Jesus and our Mother, we
believe in your triumphant assumption into Heaven where
the angels and saints acclaim you as Queen. We join them
in praising you and bless the Lord who raised you above all
creatures. With them we offer you our devotion and love.
We are confident that you watch over our daily efforts and
needs, and we take comfort from our faith in the coming
resurrection. We look to you, our life, our sweetness, and
our hope. After this earthly life, show us Jesus, the blest
fruit of your womb, Oh kind, Oh loving, Oh sweet Virgin
Mary. Amen.

ACKNOWLEDGMENTS

This book is complete because of the help and support of wonderful people to whom I am deeply grateful. First, I wish to thank Michael Lee Allen and Jill Kramer for their help in selecting and editing the true stories that appear in this book. They were both angels who gave me much-needed support and assistance—thank you!

Second, I want to send thank-yous to all of the men and women who submitted their true stories about Mother Mary to me. I admire your courage in openly discussing your deeply personal experiences, and I realize you agreed to publicly publish your stories so that others may benefit. Thank you!

Third, I want to thank those who have helped me visit the Mother Mary shrines over the years, including most recently Sonia Rossi, who took me to the Loreto Cathedral in Italy. I also wish to thank everyone at Hay House, my publishing family since 1993.

Most of all, my gratitude to God, Jesus, Mother Mary, and the angels for watching over us all and helping us to be loving and strong.

— **Doreen**

ABOUT THE AUTHOR

Doreen Virtue holds BA, MA and PhD degrees in counseling psychology. She has traveled to Marian sites internationally, including the Lourdes Grotto in France and the Loreto Cathedral in Italy. She is the author of more than 50 books and oracle card decks including *Healing with the Angels*; *Solomon's Angels*; *Archangels & Ascended Masters*; and *Angel Therapy*®, among other works. Her products are available in most languages worldwide.

Doreen has appeared on *Oprah*, CNN, *The View*, and other television and radio programmes. You can listen to Doreen's live weekly radio show, and call her for a reading, by visiting HayHouseRadio.com®.

www.angeltherapy.com

NOTES

NOTES

NOTES

NOTES

NOTES

NOTES

NOTES

NOTES

NOTES

NOTES

Hay House Titles of Related Interest

YOU CAN HEAL YOUR LIFE, the movie,
starring Louise L. Hay & Friends
(available as a 1-DVD program and an expanded 2-DVD set)
Watch the trailer at: **www.LouiseHayMovie.com**

THE SHIFT, the movie, starring Dr Wayne W. Dyer
(available as a 1-DVD program and an expanded 2-DVD set)
Watch the trailer at: **www.DyerMovie.com**

ॐ

*THE DIVINE NAME: The Sound That Can Change
the World,* by Jonathan Goldman (book-with-CD)

*FOR LOVERS OF GOD EVERYWHERE:
Poems of the Christian Mystics,* by Roger Housden

MY ANGEL DIARY 2013, by Jenny Smedley

*OUR LADY OF KIBEHO: Mary Speaks to the World from
the Heart of Africa,* by Immaculée Ilibagiza, with Steve Erwin

*PROTECTED BY ANGELS: Magical True Stories of Angelic
Intervention,* by Jacky Newcomb

*WISHES FULFILLED: Mastering the Art
of Manifesting,* by Dr Wayne W. Dyer

All of the above are available at your local bookstore,
or may be ordered by contacting Hay House (see next page).

ॐ

We hope you enjoyed this Hay House book.
If you would like to receive a free catalogue featuring additional
Hay House books and products, or if you would like information
about the Hay Foundation, please contact:

Hay House UK Ltd
292B Kensal Road • London W10 5BE
Tel: (44) 20 8962 1230; Fax: (44) 20 8962 1239
www.hayhouse.co.uk

***

Published and distributed in the United States of America by:
Hay House, Inc. • PO Box 5100 • Carlsbad, CA 92018-5100
Tel: (1) 760 431 7695 or (1) 800 654 5126;
Fax: (1) 760 431 6948 or (1) 800 650 5115
www.hayhouse.com

***

Published and distributed in Australia by:
Hay House Australia Ltd • 18/36 Ralph Street • Alexandria, NSW 2015
Tel: (61) 2 9669 4299, Fax: (61) 2 9669 4144
www.hayhouse.com.au

***

Published and distributed in the Republic of South Africa by:
Hay House SA (Pty) Ltd • PO Box 990 • Witkoppen 2068
Tel/Fax: (27) 11 467 8904
www.hayhouse.co.za

***

Published and distributed in India by:
Hay House Publishers India • Muskaan Complex • Plot No.3
B-2• Vasant Kunj • New Delhi - 110 070
Tel: (91) 11 41761620; Fax: (91) 11 41761630
www.hayhouse.co.in

***

Distributed in Canada by:
Raincoast • 9050 Shaughnessy St • Vancouver, BC V6P 6E5
Tel: (1) 604 323 7100
Fax: (1) 604 323 2600

***

Sign up via the Hay House UK website to receive the Hay House
online newsletter and stay informed about what's going on with your
favourite authors. You'll receive bimonthly announcements
about discounts and offers, special events, product highlights,
free excerpts, giveaways, and more!
www.hayhouse.co.uk